To: Casey Chandler Brogdon
1734 Scenic Highway North
Snellville, Georgia 30078

You may be too busy
living life to take time
out reading about it.

From: Edwin, The Canna Lily
Capitalist of Brogdon Siding
June 1, 2004 — Tuesday —

Brick Street Coffee Break
9 Caldwell Street
Sumter, S.C. 29150

THE LAST MAGIC SUMMER

Books by Peter Gent

North Dallas Forty

Texas Celebrity Turkey Trot

The Franchise

North Dallas After Forty

The Conquering Heroes

The Last Magic Summer

THE LAST MAGIC SUMMER

A Season with My Son
A MEMOIR

PETER GENT

William Morrow and Company, Inc. New York

Gent, Peter.
    The last magic summer : a season with my son : a memoir / by Peter Gent.
        p.   cm.
        ISBN 0-688-13365-7
        1. Youth league baseball—Michigan—Bangor. 2. Fathers and sons—Michigan—Bangor. 3. Baseball—Coaching—Michigan—Bangor. 4. Gent, Peter. 5. Gent, Carter. I. Title.
    GV880.8.G46   1996
    796.357'63'097413—dc20   95-45076
                                                                              CIP

Printed in the United States of America

First Edition

1 2 3 4 5 6 7 8 9 10

BOOK DESIGN BY LEAH CARLSON

This book is for Carter and his grandmother Elizabeth Gent, whose love and caring made all things possible. For the Bangor Connie Mack Team. And, remembering Mike Guldan (1915–1995), a constant friend.

Acknowledgments

This book could not have been completed without the selfless help and encouragement of many people, probably more than I will remember to list here.

My brother Jamie who offered support and advice on how to build and hold a team together. Jamie's wife, Cindy, who took the time to read early drafts of this work.

Dr. Michael Graf of Kalamazoo and his assistant, Jan Haak, who took special time and effort to help me deal with the physical and mental pain inflicted by years of professional football and parenthood.

Messrs C. Reid Hudgins III, Esq., and Robert B. Borsos, Esq., legal assistant Debbie Sill, and the staff of the legal firm Kreis, Enderle, Callander and Hudgins in Kalamazoo, Michigan.

C.P.A. John Donaldson, who somehow keeps the numbers right.

Paul Bresnick and Jon Moskowitz of William Morrow.

And, my deepest and most heartfelt appreciation to Sterling Lord, friend and literary agent for twenty-five years, who has worked long and hard to keep me upright as I stepped blindly into the maelstrom of the future, time after time, to try to build a life out of the chaos. A quarter century of hard work is remembered and, who knows, I may get it right yet.

My mother groan'd! my father wept.
Into the dangerous world I leapt:
Helpless, naked, piping loud,
Like a fiend hid in a cloud.

—WILLIAM BLAKE

Rays of overlooked sunshine reflect off
broken glass, an uncaring passerby,
for a reason unbeknownst to me, kicks
the shattered hopes across a busy street
and into a sewer drain, where it will
remain lonely for its sole companion,
which it so foolishly thought could
never be taken away.

—CARTER GENT, *age eleven*

PART◇ONE

Things Fall Apart

Down these mean streets a man must go. . . .
He is a common man, or he could not go among common people.
He has a sense of character, or he would not know his job.

—RAYMOND CHANDLER

The Bangor Connie Mack Roster—June 1993

Name	Pos.	Bat.	Thr.	Age	Ht.	Wt.	High School
Chris Christian	2	L	R	18	5'9"	160	Bangor
Shaun Eisner	9	R	R	18	5'11"	185	Bangor
Ben Finch	7	R	R	18	5'10"	155	Bangor
Eric Finch	4	R	R	18	6'	175	Bangor
Mike Fusco	6	R	R	18	6'	155	Decatur
Carter Gent	8	R	R	17	6'2"	160	Bangor
Greg Grosvenor	5/1	R	R	18	5'11"	195	Decatur
Steve Leonard	9	R	R	18	5'10"	170	Bangor
Brian Seymour	1	R	R	17	5'9"	150	Bangor
Mike Wisniewski	1/5	L	L	17	5'11"	165	Bangor
Mike Wisser	1/3	R	R	18	6'2"	175	Bangor

1 ◇ July 23, 1992—The Playoff Game

This ain't competition, man,
this is war
And you can't hit the corners no more.
—BOB SEGER, *"Can't Hit the Corners"*

I WAS SICK WITH anxiety. We were losing! This was *it*! Bangor versus Kalamazoo Too in Bangor, July 23, 1992.

After winning five of six of our regular season Connie Mack games against Kalamazoo Too, this "playoff game" had been forced on us by league director and Kalamazoo Maroons Organization general manager Mike Hinga. I was pissed and I was scared.

My son, Carter, was coming up to bat. We were behind, 4–3, in the bottom of the sixth with one out and a man on second. All our work. The whole season coming down to this seven-inning game and the pressure was on Carter to deliver.

I was not at all happy about having to play this game. At a meeting earlier in the week, I had argued against it with Mike Hinga. My position was that we had already won the right to a spot in the 1992 American Amateur Baseball Congress Connie Mack State District Tournament on the basis of our taking five of six from Kalamazoo Too. Mike said he had refigured the season using a different win-loss formula and we had to have this "playoff game." It was a one-sided discussion. The Double-header League was his league. Not only was he league director, but as general manager of the Kalamazoo Maroons AABC Organization, Mike had overall responsibility for the other three teams in the league.

All three teams, the Maroons, Kalamazoo Too, and RATHCO,

(named after the company that sponsored it), wore Maroons uniforms. His three votes against my one. He had me mouse-trapped. The meeting was simply a pretense that we were having a reasonable discussion, reaching an amicable compromise. Fait accompli, I had lost before I started. Outsmarted. Outmaneu-vered. Outcoached. Pure Baseball. Can't hit the corners? Rede-fine the corners. It ain't cheating if you don't get caught.

So, we had to beat Kalamazoo Too, again. Six out of seven? This was proving a very difficult task. These guys were good baseball players. They had already beat the Maroons once and tied them once.

Man for man, I thought my kids were better but we lacked KTOO's depth. And we were tired. Carter and his Bangor team-mates had spent the day getting the field into playing shape. They were moving water, shoveling mud, spreading sand and crushed rock, and lining the field all day long. Meanwhile, the Kalamazoo Too kids rested at home. It had poured all the night before and nobody from the Bangor Summer Recreation Pro-gram could be bothered to repair the field. It was their job. They had the proper equipment. They got paid money for doing it. But I could not get them to do anything but frown and shake their heads.

Since the kids had worked all day in ninety-degree heat, they started tired, without a keen edge and concentration—hell, I was tired and all I had done was watch them work—now, we had big trouble with Kalamazoo Too.

Their Greg Grosvenor had been throwing well and had scat-tered our hits.

If we lost this game to the number two team in the Kalamazoo Maroons Connie Mack Organization, we would fail to qualify for the state district tournament. The alternative was to cancel and I knew that meant Mike Hinga would declare us forfeit and KTOO would get the district tournament seed. (Mike was also the AABC Connie Mack tournament director for our state district.)

My team. My kids. My son. I tried to look out for their interests and protect their rights. But Hinga had to do the same thing for his teams and he had sixty kids who paid around three or four hundred dollars apiece to play. At those prices, parents wanted winners. They certainly would be upset if their kids kept getting spanked by this little hillbilly town of eighteen hundred people from the swamp thirty miles west on the road to Lake Michigan. I had twelve kids who paid eight dollars apiece *if* they had it. Many didn't and Carter's grandmother often made up the difference out of her small pension, Social Security, and decreasing savings. The Maroons organization's success was Hinga's responsibility and Mike knew baseball. I was overmatched.

My twelve Bangor kids had talent. But they all had jobs and little time to practice; and they didn't even have uniforms. Besides, what did I know about coaching the Connie Mack level of baseball with all its pitching, hitting, and baserunning strategies?

I had played Big-Ten basketball at Michigan State and NFL football for the Dallas Cowboys. I hadn't played baseball in over thirty-five years since high school. I didn't even follow baseball. Figuring out free substitutions and the designated hitter rule was like trying to do Chinese arithmetic.

Over the years, major league baseball players had become my friends and acquaintances. We talked about women, drinking, and each other; we told road trip anecdotes and locker room jokes. We never talked about the strategies and tactics of baseball or football.

Carter was at bat, batting seventh in the lineup. He had been hitting the ball, but KTOO was a good defensive team and he had yet to reach base. I was feeling queasy.

Shaun Eisner had singled, then reached second base on Josh Carpenter's sacrifice bunt. Everybody in our dugout was up on his feet screaming.

The KTOO players were confident all-star players chosen from the Kalamazoo area and southwestern Michigan high schools. Many were all-conference, all-district, all-region, and all-state players at their respective schools. They were instructed by qualified baseball coaches in a summer-long program of daily practices and teaching sessions. They were outfitted with top-of-the-line equipment.

KTOO scored all four of their runs in the first inning against our left-hander Mike "Nuke" Wisniewski on three hits, one walk, and two errors.

Nuke doesn't give up four runs in a game. They happened in the first inning when he was just starting to recover from working on the field. And since that inning, Wisniewski had shut them down. Tired as they were, the Bangor kids were reaching down inside for that something extra. They had better find it . . . fast.

Carter dug in as KTOO pitcher Grosvenor wound up and rocketed a BB in low at the knees. Carter took a called strike. It was a strike all the way and he knew it. But it wasn't the pitch he wanted and he didn't waste a swing. He clenched his jaws and concentrated to keep the fear controlled.

Out there all alone. My heart ached for him.

After all Carter had gone through, God now had him on baseball's anvil and appeared set to pulverize his ego, pounding humiliation into the depths of his soul, pitch by agonizing pitch. I didn't know if I could stand to watch.

He had to get a hit. It meant so much to him to do well for his teammates. They would do the same for him and he knew it. These kids loved each other.

"No hitter up there, Greg baby. No batter. This guy is nothing. Bring the heat. Blow him out." The KTOO players were reassuring Grosvenor, who had a good fastball and a curve.

"Just meet the ball, Carter. Get it started. Bring Shaun around. We need this, Carter," the Bangor players were calling out to him.

Grosvenor was a big right-handed pitcher, on the short side of two hundred pounds. He seemed to leap off the mound at the batter with a terrifying delivery. An impressive pitcher, he already had seven strikeouts.

Tall and slender, Carter looked so fragile and so hopelessly alone at the plate, the Kalamazoo Too pitcher could kill my kid and it would be my fault.

Grosvenor started his stretch. I had to force myself to watch.

A right-handed batter, Carter stayed loose in the box until Grosvenor started his motion, then he locked himself into a crouch with his bat pulled back low above and behind his shoulder.

Lunging off the mound with an audible grunt, Grosvenor gambled and tried to blow another pitch by Carter. The fastball streaked right down the pipe.

Carter saw it coming all the way, the pitch he wanted, the one he was waiting for, and his timing was perfect. Striding out smoothly, he kept his head on the ball and took a full cut. Right on the ball, Carter could drive it straightaway center field for extra bases, because the KTOO outfielders were cheating in to make sure a single didn't score Shaun Eisner with the tying run from second base.

Carter made contact. But, still arm-sore from ten hours of raking, shoveling, and working the rain-soaked field, he let his back elbow drop ever so slightly. The bat sliced under the ball fouling it off behind our dugout.

KTOO's players went crazy.

"No hitter, Greg baby, no stick. Take him out."

Grosvenor sighed and allowed himself to relax. A smart, savvy player from nearby Decatur, he knew he had gotten lucky.

Now the count was 0 and 2. My heart hammered against my rib cage.

Wisniewski stared out at the field like a recon Marine—his eyes vacant, seeing beyond. He wanted this win bad. He had worked hard for it. He hated losing.

If only Carter could get a hit.

2 ◇ Carter—1993

Excerpt from a letter from league director Mike Hinga, June 1993:

> *The Kalamazoo Connie Mack League Rules and Regulations*
> *Managers:*
> *Enclosed is the final revised schedule. Please note the addition*
> *of Gull Lake to our league. . . .*
> *Thanks*
> *Mike Hinga*

KALAMAZOO CONNIE MACK LEAGUE
JUNE 19, 1993

West Division

1. Kalamazoo Maroons	5. Kalamazoo Too
3. Bangor	4. Paw Paw

East Division

2. Gull Lake	6. Galesburg
7. Coldwater	8. Colon

Team at Large: 9. RATHCO

There was more stuff in the letter about AABC entry fees, when and how the game balls were to be obtained, and the umpires to be paid. And, of course, the schedule.

But that first paragraph gave the most important information, except for the fact that Galesburg had dropped out of the East Division, making it a three-team division and immediately bringing into question how the teams from the league would qualify for the District Tournament. Wins and Losses? Points?

Because of Rule K.

3 points are awarded for a victory over a team in your divi-
sion, 2 points for a victory over a team in the other division,
1 point for a tie, ½ point for a loss, and 0 points for a game
not played. Standings and division winners will be determined
by total points. Games with RATHCO will count in the league
standings [as nondivisional games]. RATHCO plays each
league member 1 Doubleheader and will split the umpires always.

One half point for a loss and no points for a forfeit or a rainout? The hairs on my neck stood up. What did that mean?

As I finished reading Rule K, Carter walked up on the porch of my office. Tall and lean, he had brown eyes and thick brown hair. His slender build made him look even taller. Carter had just finished high school baseball.

The high school team was good, built around the kids who had played on our Connie Mack team in the summers of 1991 and 1992. They hit well and had two good pitchers in Mike Wisser and Mike Wisniewski. They had won their high school district in Fennville and gone all the way to the regional finals before losing to the eventual state champions.

Since 1991, our first season playing at the Connie Mack level, Carter had done a lot of growing and had moved from second base into center field. He had good foot speed and a strong arm, and had perfected his batting stance and swing which gave him an average of around .350.

"Hey, Dad." Carter loped through the door. His brown hair fell across his high forehead.

"Hey, bub, good to see you." It *was* good to see him. Everyday it was good to see him. Whenever he walked into my office, or into his grandmother's house where we lived, my mood immediately changed for the better.

"What are you doing?" he asked, looking around my office.

"Putting the Connie Mack schedule in my word processor." I leaned back with the keyboard still in my lap. "I'll print up copies for everybody."

Stretching forward, I felt something slip in my lower spine.

My back had been killing me for months, leaving me bedridden much of the winter. Old injuries. The price I paid for old memories.

"What's the schedule like? How tough will it be?" Carter asked.

"I can't tell. It's complicated," I replied. "It seems Hinga has decided to determine standings with a point system instead of win-and-loss records."

"Lemme see." Carter walked across the room, and I handed him the schedule.

"The whole thing looks stacked against us," I said.

Carter cocked his head as he read. He studied the sheets for a while and then looked up at me. "So," he drawled at me out of the side of his mouth. "You are still . . . ah . . . the paranoid?" He was jerking me around.

"Yeah, Spike, it's my job." I waved him off. Paranoia was my province.

Carter was wound up and cooking. He was too happy to look on the downside of anything. He was excited about summer and the upcoming Connie Mack season.

I was proud of him and the rest of the team. They had worked hard toward the goals of knocking off the Maroons and Kalamazoo Too in the regular season and the state tournaments. They had had exceptional success in the regular season last summer.

Coaching summer baseball since Carter and his friends played Midget League, I had watched them get bigger and better. Seeing them grow from confused and clumsy little kids into talented and skilled young men was a pleasure I would always savor. Though coaching was too grand a title for the job. I showed them how to hold a bat, wear a glove, hit and field the ball. I wasn't a great coach but I didn't teach them bad habits and broke the ones they had picked up on their own. Most important, I showed up. I was there.

Being a coach can be rewarding and valuable, as long as you remember that the game is about the kids and not you. A coach who puts himself before the kids is on the road to madness and child abuse.

"Coldwater and Colon are about eighty miles from here, fifty miles on the other side of Kalamazoo." I continued to plow the furrows of Connie Mack conspiracy. "There is no way we can make five-thirty weekday games. Most of our kids don't get off from their summer jobs until five."

"I see we are in the same division with the Maroons, Kalamazoo Too, and Paw Paw." Carter looked up and grinned.

"That division will be the toughest," I said. "Do you care?"

"I love it." Carter's big brown eyes gleamed. "I want to play those guys. It's fun to play the Maroons. Beating them means something. Those guys got mad skills."

"I wonder who they'll have as pitchers?" I studied Carter's face.

"I heard they've got Dennis Gest and Pat Dunham this year," Carter said.

"Did they play last year?" I was looking at the Maroons's 1992 roster. "They aren't listed on last year's roster."

"Dunham throws smoke." He continued to read. "Dunham is Division One talent."

"Where did he go to school?"

"Portage Central or Northern, I think." Carter frowned in thought. "I can't remember right now. One of those schools around Kalamazoo."

"That's a lot of schools." I studied the 1992 Maroons's roster. They had players from Portage Northern and Portage Central plus Kalamazoo Loy Norrix and Kalamazoo Central, the home of Derek Jeter. These were all class A schools. Also, they had players from class B schools: Paw Paw, Three Rivers, Vicksburg, Bronson, and Comstock. Bangor was class C.

"Besides Dunham and Gest," Carter said, screwing up his mouth in a tight frown, "they'll probably have Brad Block and Eric Johnson back from Portage Central, Josh Cooper from Comstock, Scott Wetherbee from Loy Norrix, and Laskovy from Paw Paw."

"How do you remember all the names?" I asked.

"All the Maroons are good." He smiled. "You remember good players."

I read through the previous year's Maroons roster. Of the eighteen players listed, all were seventeen or eighteen, eleven had already graduated from high school, six would graduate this year and one in 1994.

On the other hand, our 1992 team had two players who had already graduated, and the remainder were evenly split between sixteen- and seventeen-year-olds, except Eric Buskirk who was only fifteen.

"Didn't Laskovy pitch for Kalamazoo Too last year? " I asked.

"Yeah, he's not bad but we roped him," Carter said. "He was that big tall kid that always had that huge dip of snuff under his lower lip."

Carter's once chubby face was now dominated by bone structure. A full high forehead sloped into brows that softened the prominent ridgeline divided by his strong, straight nose. When you looked at him, it was still not hard to see the little boy somewhere in there. The child beneath the young man.

"You like my 'stache?" He caught me staring and smoothed the thin line of hair on his upper lip with his thumb and forefinger. Soft dark facial hair, not a heavy growth of bristle.

"Yeah." I nodded.

At least, he hadn't gotten his ears or nose pierced or talked about getting nipple rings. It was those little things a father grows more and more thankful for as he ages.

Carter was growing a mustache. Time was passing quickly. I wanted this coming summer to last forever. Hell, I wanted this day to last forever. I was scared, frightened of the day he would go to college and move on with his life. The next big move he made would be without me.

He would grow up. I would grow old. Maybe.

Actuarial studies of the life expectancy of ex-professional football players were not encouraging. The more recent numbers had my generation of NFL players heading for that big huddle in the sky at about sixty-one years old. I was already fifty-one. Guys I had played with and against were already dead, some for over a decade. If I was a cynic, I would say the sixty-one-year life expectancy could be why my NFLPA death benefit with Carter as beneficiary ended at fifty-five.

I was a cynic.

The NFL and the NFLPA had no health plan and not much of a pension for retired players from my era. Somehow all the whining and striking benefited only the union and the current active players at the cost of those of us who had gone before. If I took retirement at fifty-one, my monthly pension would be $240 dollars a month. At fifty-five it would be $335. I would get $877 a month if I waited until sixty-five. That was four years after I was expected to die. Death would make cashing the checks difficult. My dealings with the owners and union nurtured the fear that if I didn't die at sixty-one, they would send somebody out to kill me.

The thought of my small pension and what it boded for Carter's future and mine was not a pleasant thought. The guilt of past mistakes had never left me once in the ten years since my divorce had buried me in debt and joined me at the hip with the IRS.

Suddenly depression was clouding over what had begun as a beautiful spring day with Carter. I told myself that things would get better and this too would pass. But what had passed had been Carter's childhood. As he moved into young adulthood, I was still unable to earn enough money to guarantee he would have the necessary education to survive in the ruins of post-Reagan Bush America. The financial bulwark I had built around my family had been washed away in the ugly flood of divorce and custody litigation in the early eighties. With such behavior, adults spend a childhood.

"Take a closer look at Rule K," I said to Carter.

He sat down on the trundle bed next to the fireplace and read.

"Why points instead of win-loss records?" Carter asked. "And, why are wins in our division worth three points while all others are worth two?"

"Exactly," I said. "Who qualifies for the District Tournament? Division winners? The teams with the most points? Plus, Galesburg has dropped out of the East Division."

"The East is a three-team division?" Carter paused to consider the math. He looked out the window toward the blinking light at the corner of Center and Monroe streets. "That has to hurt Coldwater, Gull Lake, and Colon with fewer wins worth three points."

"I know, I just got off the phone with Dave Martin, the coach in Coldwater. He's going to call Hinga to get a clarification."

"Why don't you call Hinga?"

"No deal. I haven't recovered from last year's 'discussion' over that 'playoff' game with Kalamazoo Too," I said. "Mike's smart. He'll mousetrap me again just like last summer."

"Oh . . . yeah . . . that game." Carter clasped his hands behind his head. A tight grimace pulled at his lips and tiny crow's-feet spread at the corners of his eyes. "What a bitch of a day that was."

"That game gave me a two-day headache. I smoked a hundred cigarettes and screamed 'atta boy' a thousand times." Leaning back in my chair to ease the tension in my back, I laced my fingers and locked my hands behind my head.

"Don't forget all the times you yelled 'steal!' " Carter smirked.

"I had to yell 'steal!' " I turned defensive. "We never had one practice because most of the kids worked. When were we gonna get time to work on baserunning signals?"

"Yelling 'steal!' seemed to work." Carter grinned. "Nobody thought we would be stupid enough to actually yell out our signals to our base runners."

After reading Rule K again, he looked at me.

"Why would a team get half a point for losing and nothing for a game not played?" Carter asked.

"Sounds kind of shifty, doesn't it?" I saw plots against me everywhere. "I asked Dave Martin to find out about that too. He sounds like a good guy. Your uncle Jamie knows him."

My younger brother, Jamie, had been a teacher-coach at Haslett High School outside East Lansing ever since he finished his football career and graduated from Central Michigan University in 1967. He had recently taken the athletic director's job.

Stretched out on the trundle bed, Carter stared up at the ceiling. His size-ten feet hung off the end of the bed. He was wearing a pair of Nikes that cost more than my first car. His grandmother had bought them for him.

My back was killing me, as it had for over twenty-five years. Too many headgears in the spine while going across the middle on third down for long yardage and short money for the Cowboys. The last days of the old NFL before the merger, big money, steroids, cocaine, and the contamination of the gene pool.

"What are you doing today?" I asked Carter.

"Chris Christian, Mike Wisser, Steve Leonard, and the Finch twins are going over to use the pitching machines and batting cages in Paw Paw." Carter frowned. He was agitated. "We've been trying to find Mike Wisniewski to go with us."

They organized their own practices. Since I was too crippled to swing a bat or throw a ball, I was little help. My job was basically to be the "responsible adult" who attended league meetings and maintained dialogues with other coaches to double-check game times and umpires and to reschedule games when necessary.

"Isn't Wisniewski at home?" I asked.

"Not for a couple days." Carter got up and paced the office.

Nuke Wisniewski's personal problems were tidal: They ebbed and flowed. His parents had had an unhappy, violent marriage and his mother had moved to Bangor to escape, that and the violence from Chicago's gangs. Although he was a tough kid who took shit from no one, Mike had the clothes stolen off his back and the shoes off his feet at gunpoint by gang bangers. The brutality he had seen was still visible in his eyes, if you looked to find it.

I liked Mike. He was a great player, a left-handed pitching phenom—and, like my son and most of his teammates, a damaged kid.

"I left a message," Carter said. "If he gets it he'll be there. Mike loves to play baseball."

Carter flopped down in the gray armchair across from my working table and peered at me over the piles of paper, envelopes, and junk. He handed me a sheaf of papers. "We got our stats for this high school season," he said.

"You batted .359." I read through them. "Had seventeen RBIs in twenty-six games. That's pretty good."

"I did okay."

"I read in the *Kalamazoo Gazette* today that the Yankees expect big things from Derek Jeter," I said. "He's in their farm system playing down in Greensboro."

"Yeah, I know. He was the first high school kid picked in the 1992 draft when he was still playing for the Maroons." Carter's eyes clicked out of focus. He was thinking about Jeter. "I loved playing against him. He's going to be a major star. Remember, I told you first"—Carter raised his voice to make certain I heard—"Derek Jeter is going to be one of the great all-time major league players."

"I'll remember," I said.

Derek Jeter from Kalamazoo had been picked the National High School Baseball Player of the Year in 1992. Carter had played against him in Connie Mack in the summers of 1991 and 1992.

A year later Jeter was in Triple A Columbus and Minor League Player of the Year. By May 1995, he was playing shortstop for the Yankees. At twenty years of age, Jeter was the youngest player in the American League and the second youngest starter in history to wear the pinstripes.

"Steinbrenner said Jeter had a good bat and was a sure bet for the major leagues."

I bit back the cynical observation that seemed so clear to me. Derek Jeter was a first-class kid: decent, hardworking, and talented. But after years of dedication and sacrifice had brought him to the doorstep of the major leagues, his future in baseball depended on the iron whim of George Steinbrenner. (In June 1995, confirming my worst opinions of owners and George Steinbrenner in particular, Steinbrenner added a questionable Darryl Strawberry to the roster and sent Jeter, who was hitting with power and had a respectable average, back down to triple A Columbus.)

Carter accurately predicted the futures of players in all sports. That spring of 1993, Carter said a running back at San Diego State, Marshall Faulk, was a sure future NFL star over every other college back in the nation. And in 1994 Faulk would star as a rookie for the Indianapolis Colts.

Carter continued, "The Kalamazoo Maroons were a great team that first year we played them in the State Districts. They had Jeter, Ryan Topham, and Shane Sheldon. All of them heading for the pros. It was just great to play against them." (Topham would bypass the high school draft and go to Notre Dame on scholarship. During his 1995 junior year he would be an NCAA leader with a .365 batting average, eighteen home runs, and eighty RBIs. And, within just a few days of his ex-Maroons teammate Derek Jeter moving up to a starting position with the Yankees, Ryan Topham would be selected by the Chicago White Sox in the fourth round. In September 1995 the Yankees would bring Derek Jeter back up for their *abortive* run at the American League Pennant.)

Carter dropped a piece of paper on my filing cabinet.

"What's that?" I asked.

"My certificate for winning a baseball letter last year."

"And you just got it?"

He nodded. I didn't say any more.

Carter lost patience with me when I got angry at these oversights by the high school coaches and administrators. But lately, I was short-tempered. Blaming others. I went to bed scared, tossed and turned scared, then got up in the morning tired and scared and feeling guilty.

Time was running out. I had to do something right. This coming summer had to bring some good news, some accomplishment, and maybe just a little magic. This was the last summer . . . my last chance. It was a fearful thing to have lost my son's future and, growing old, know the time for me to earn it back was nearly gone. The chances for success slimmer and slimmer.

Starved for hope, I searched for the answers. But, as I grew old there were fewer adults whose wisdom I trusted.

It had become *my* job to be wise. My responsibility was to pass on my wisdom to Carter. What wisdom? Carter's mother and I had literally slashed and burned his future in front of his eyes.

"Are we finally gonna have uniforms this year?" Carter asked. "It'd be nice to look like a team instead of a bunch of migrant workers."

"I'll call your uncle Jamie. He'll know how to get uniforms and what they'll cost," I said. "The problem is money. I hate asking people for money. 'I'll pay you back' is going to be my epitaph."

"You're always talking about how Tony Eicas and Grandpa got money for you guys in high school; maybe Tony'll help us," said Carter, heading into the next room.

My office was in an old Victorian house, originally the Bangor parish rectory for the Sacred Heart Catholic Church. It was a classic old house with eleven rooms, two baths, a full basement, a fireplace, expensive hand-tooled woodwork, hundred-year-old beveled-glass windows, and hot-water heat.

Carter had only been a year old when we left Michigan for Texas in October 1977. His sister, Holly, was fourteen, and his mother and I were still married. Battered and worn out, only Carter and I came back to Bangor in October 1985. Returning to my old hometown gave me scores of friends and neighbors who helped me, as a single parent, keep track of Carter as a matter of routine.

Shortly after returning, I rented an office in the parish house from Angelo Distefano. Angelo and his brother Andy owned and operated Distefano's Amoco station on the corner of Monroe and Center streets, at the blinking light, near the heart of downtown Bangor. Carter and I lived one block south of my office on Center Street with Carter's grandmother in the house where my two brothers and I had grown up.

3 ◇ "The Purple Virus" by CARTER, age eight

AUGUST 17, 1984

There were two people who had bad viruses. They went to many Doc.

None of them could figure it out. But finally a doc. figured it out. It was called the purple virus. It had killed many people. It would take 24 days to make a medicine.

The wife died fast. The father did not know what to do.

Finally the phone rang. It was the Doc.

He could not have the cure for six months.

"I can not stay a live for that long."

"Then you have to go in to Dead Mill to get some yellow water.

"Are you brave enough to do it?"

"Yes of course for my life."

"Ok have it your way."

"Good bye."

"Good bye."

So he goes he finds the yellow water. The yellow water was hot. He heard a strange noise. Like a growling sound. It was a big dragon!

He ran for his life! The dragon blew fire at him! He cried help! help! Nobody heard him.

The dragon was close behind. He was in trouble. He was scared to death. "help! help!" he yelled again.

Finnaly he was out of the cave. "Man oh man!"

"Well I might as well drink it."

It was dark by then. The dragon was still after him. He was traped. He screamd there was no noise.

The next day they found him alive. They took him away to the hospital. He was there six months.

They had the cure for purple virus.

Everybody was happy. itsept the guy oh lost his wife.

He was sad. The people tried to cheer him up. But he kept looking sad.

Someone asked whats a mater.

No ansawer.

4 ◊ The Texas Diaries—1983

The protection of the Law is too severe an ordeal for poor human nature . . . the man who habituates himself to this distortion of Truth and to exultation at the success of injustice will, at last, hardly know right from wrong.

—NAPOLEON, FROM ELBA

I ALWAYS ASSUMED "The Purple Virus" story was Carter's way of putting the insanity of his parents' divorce into perspective. The Purple Virus. The plague of human behavior. We never found a cure and it took us nearly three years to escape, badly burned, from the dragon of Dead Mill.

The long financial and emotional siege began when his mother disappeared from our house in the Texas hill country community of Wimberley in the early-morning hours of January 30, 1983. She up and vanished in the middle of a sudden, unexpected argument. Her behavior appeared more impulsive than it actually was but that was a hard lesson I was to learn later.

That particular January night, I had been working for two days

and nights without pause, trying to finish a novel by early February. After working constantly for nearly two years, I was within
a couple of weeks of finishing. The work had taken a terrible
toll on all of us. And somehow the dragon had been awakened
and I stumbled right into it while making coffee to keep me
going until dawn.

My wife walked into the kitchen. I was sitting on the floor
waiting for the water to boil. She had just turned thirty-seven
and for the past several years had been troubled that she did
not have a career of her own.

I took her unhappiness seriously but felt this was something I
could put off dealing with until after I had finished the book.
Wrong. Thirty-seven is a dangerous age for a married woman
who had been on the fringes of the fast lanes of athletic fame,
New York publishing, and Hollywood movies for fifteen years
because she was married to some man who was now spending
months locked up with his typewriter while she was closing the
gap on forty.

"You'll have to pick up Carter at school tomorrow," she told
me as I sat on the carpet. "I have a doctor's appointment."

"What's wrong?" I shifted my weight on the floor and leaned
against the cupboard doors.

"I'm having a problem with Carter."

"Why aren't you taking him to the doctor if he's got a
problem?"

"Well ... because ... it's about Carter ... but ..." she was
having trouble articulating.

"What's going on?" I asked. I was anxious to cut to the chase
and get back to work.

"I am having trouble dealing with Carter. I am going to see
a psychologist. She's on staff at Southwest Texas State."

The word "psychologist" sent shivers up my spine. She had
excused some horrible behavior in her past before I met her
by saying "a psychologist had told me it was the best thing to
do." What was she up to now? Her process of seeking professional advice was to go from one "expert" to the next until she

finally found one who would agree with the decision she had already made.

What was this problem with Carter? Carter was a really good kid. He was mannerly and highly intelligent; he behaved himself and never caused trouble. She really hadn't been around Carter that much, anyway. Lately, she was gone from the house most of the time. She spent long afternoons and evenings in Austin while I worked. She would call saying she could not get back to pick up Carter from school and that I had to get him and watch him until she got home—later than expected. Often, after school, she would leave Carter with his playmates, forcing their parents to become de facto baby-sitters.

She was bored and thought she was being cheated out of something. She said that she wanted "more." The eighties were in full bloom, a decade-long party was on, there was money to burn, and she wanted her rightful place at the fire.

After over twenty years off and on the fast lane of pro football, publishing, television, and movies, I had learned some painful lessons. I was reluctant to even leave the house until the book was finished. But by turning down my spot near the fire, I became a candidate as fuel.

"It'll help me be a better parent and add to my life," she said, pressing to see the psychologist. "I want a career."

"A career takes years of hard work," I said. "People study and work for years, and then maybe, maybe, they have a career." She was capable of the work; it was the choice of work I worried about.

"That's what I want to do," she replied. "I'd like to paint. Or, maybe go to college or get a license to sell real estate."

Sell real estate? That was just beautiful. People everywhere in Texas in the eighties were selling real estate, if they weren't brokering crooked oil deals and bankrupting savings and loans.

"Painting or selling real estate?" I said. "Your first problem is obviously making a career choice. What about the circus?"

"The problems are just as much yours as mine," she said.

"I believe you," I replied sharply. "But making a decision this big in the middle of the night a couple of weeks before I finish twenty-two months' work on a book is insane.''

"What is the sense in waiting?'' she snapped.

"We'll be rested, calmer, and under a lot of less pressure,'' I replied. "I don't want to have this argument again with you now. We have a twenty-year-old daughter and a six-year-old son. Their problems come way ahead of yours,'' I snorted derisively. "Painting or selling real estate, Christ on a rubber crutch.'' It was a cheap shot and not the way to search for a better understanding of the problem. On the other hand, it was true and suddenly I was angry.

"Look, you better get your shit together.'' I was raising my voice geometrically with each thought. I knew what she was up to, at least, I thought I did. She would tell the "expert'' a story designed to get the psychologist to confirm decisions made long ago. "You aren't going to some cut-rate college psychologist to put my business in the street so you can feel better about yourself. Nobody is dining out in San Marcos on our family's private life.''

"I have a life too,'' she began to argue back.

"Look, we're tired and angry. This is not the time.'' I struggled to calm down and failed.

"You can't control me forever,'' she said.

Control me! Those were not her words. She didn't think or talk in that manner. She was aping somebody.

"Nobody is controlling you and you know it. Is that what you've been doing everyday these past weeks? Going off and complaining to one of your 'new' friends about how you are controlled by the big bad ex-football player?'' She was definitely up to no good. But I was just too tired to think this through. Unfortunately as well, the objects in my subconscious were closer than they appeared.

"I have been doing no such thing,'' she said. Her eyes told a different story. She seemed to be gauging the distances between me, her, and the various doors.

"I am warning you,'' I said. Now I was furious, realizing that she was actually spending her time conspiring and complaining about her difficult life. "Start a fight with me now and it will go thermonuclear. Because I got some beefs of my own about your recent behavior."

It was a stupid, macho thing to say. The devil made me do it. But the remark struck home, set her in a panic, and led to loud recriminations. We both raised our voices. Understanding was gone, if it had ever been there.

Afraid that we had awakened Carter, I got up and walked back into our bedroom, where I found him asleep. When I returned to the kitchen, it was empty. My wife was gone in her car. It was late at night, but we had friends living nearby and I didn't think she was in danger.

She wasn't. Carter and I were.

She had been spending her time complaining. I was right about that. But that was all I had right.

I did not know that she already had a bag packed, had been consulting a divorce lawyer, and was set to transfer all the monies from our joint accounts to secret accounts she had opened. She took all the cash, book and film contracts, car and house titles, land deeds, gold coins, silver bars, certificates of deposit, jewelry, and the safe-deposit box keys.

This wasn't about right or wrong, good or bad. This was about power and who was going to exercise it. Truth gave way quickly to lies, because there is no greater exercise of power than the ability to define reality. It was, and had always been, a struggle for control, driven by the volatile dynamics of family politics and her desire to empower herself. Agonizing and dangerous emotions boiled to overflowing, making Carter and his sister the victims of psychological violence and emotional pain.

Nothing hurt like this, before or since.

The only analgesic I found that seemed to mitigate the damage was to encourage Carter to play baseball. The pastoral peace, slow pace, the socialization and bonding possibilities of the long periods spent on the field and in the dugout, seemed healthy and healing. Escaping into our games, Carter and I survived. Using a wadded sock as a ball and a rolled-up newspaper for a bat, we played in hotel and motel rooms from the San Marcos and Austin, Texas, Holiday Inns to the Waldorf in New York and the Westwood Marquis near UCLA on the edge of Hollywood.

We played catch outside the Quality Inn south of Austin and next to the office of the Wimberley Justice of the Peace Clarence "Sonny" Gold and the café run by his wife, Laurel. Tossing a baseball back and forth, we would wait outside the Hays County Courthouse in San Marcos, Texas, while inside lawyers and strangers portioned out our lives like slices of fatback.

Guilt or innocence entered into the long process only slightly less than truth. The courthouse was where everybody went to lie. Entering a courtroom believing in justice was to invite disaster. Domestic court battles were not about winning or losing, they were about endurance. It was about how much paper one filed, how much money one had, how much pain one was willing to inflict and how much one could stand.

In the end, Carter emerged battered but intact. He was forced to grow up in a matter of months into a tough, cagey infighter in the daily battles over who was to control his life. And, finally, he ended up controlling his life himself.

Baseball developed his understanding of people's personal strengths and weaknesses, and their strategies for empowering themselves and weakening him. He learned to study people on the playing field and in the dugout and applied that knowledge to gain some control of his fate in the politics of the broken family.

Considering he was only six when our domestic dysfunction escalated from guerrilla warfare to a full-blown public declaration of war, Carter did quite well. He survived. Now that Carter was a grown-up, it couldn't hurt him anymore. Problem was, it couldn't hurt him any less.

5 ◇ July 23, 1992—The Playoff Game

CARTER STEPPED AWAY FROM the box and looked off toward the football field and track, trying to relax, trying to concentrate, trying to find somewhere inside what he needed. The second fastball had been exactly the pitch he wanted. He should have hit that ball. His concentration was right. His technique perfect. But his back elbow had dropped. Now, down 0–2, he might never see another good pitch again.

Why did I put him seventh in the order? If he failed here, it would be all my fault. But he would never believe that. Was this what Carter got for nine years of work and dedication? Failure?

After all the times in Texas we snuck off to play catch and practice hitting, evading my ex-wife, her opportunistic and irresponsible Texas lawyer who had the ethics of . . . well . . . a Texas lawyer, and that goddamn judge with his TROs, contempt citations, arrest warrants, one-sided hearings, rulings, jail sentences—after the cruel and lunatic behavior to keep us apart, to keep me out of his life and away from his baseball games—had it all been a preface to this moment?

He had been trying to do right so hard for so long. Just sixteen, Carter had already had enough disappointment to fill two lifetimes. And now, he was one strike away from turning into the Mighty Casey.

Carter had learned that the law wasn't justice, lawyers weren't honest, and judges weren't fair. But, goddamnit baseball was supposed to be fair. Even when Mike Hinga had redefined the rules, he thought he was being fair. He didn't just give Kalamazoo Too the district seed, which he could have done. Kalamazoo Too still had to beat us. And now they were beating us.

How did it turn so bad so fast? Because it rained last night.

The Finch twins, Ben and Eric, catcher Chris Christian, pitcher

Andy Murray, first baseman/pitcher Mike Wisser, outfielders Steve Leonard and Shaun Eisner, all of them were tired. But after the first inning, Wisniewski caught his second wind and, besides shutting KTOO out, knocked in our second and third runs with a third-inning triple to left center field. Nuke's hit had bounced off the fence in the air and driven in Chris Christian and Eric Finch who had reached base with walks. Now, Shaun was waiting on second base for Carter to put the ball in play and bring him home.

I looked around the dugout and studied their faces. They looked determined, eyes bright, jaws set, fighting off the weariness, beginning to pull themselves up to the task. Behind, 4–3, with a man on, one out, and Carter up with an 0–2 count, Bangor was not finished yet.

Carter adjusted his batting gloves and I suddenly flashed back a decade to Texas and the day he asked me to get him his first pair of batting gloves . . . for Tee Ball.

"Dad, you know what I need is batting gloves." He was six years old and stood beside me on the car seat, making us the same height. His little arm slung loosely over my shoulder.

"Batting gloves for Tee Ball?"

"Yeah, they're cool, man." He was excited.

"Cool, hey, man?" I held out my right palm and he slapped me five with his tiny hand. How could I resist a chance to watch my six-year-old son adjust his batting gloves in Tee Ball? I bought the gloves.

Now, a six-foot-two Carter banged his bat against his cleats, studied the layout of the field, looked out at Grosvenor on the mound, held up one hand signaling time-out, and stepped slowly back into the batter's box. Then . . . he stepped back out and looked over at his teammates in the dugout, took a deep breath, and exhaled, raising his eyebrows and nodding his head just slightly.

"Come on, Carter, goddamnit!" Mike Wisniewski shouted in his high, nasal Chicago accent. "You can hit that ball. Let's go. I didn't do all this shit to lose to these guys."

"That's right, Carter!" Mike Wisser, the once and future vale-
dictorian added, his tone strangely logical, almost academic.
This was math. This was science. This was art. This was war. This
was baseball and to these kids it all made perfect sense. Baseball
was order when all else was chaos.

Inside our dugout, these young men knew it was now or never.
They knew they were capable of winning this game. Because
they were kids, they were capable of a lot more than that. That's
what kids are about, making the impossible possible. The mira-
cle of youth, creating the future. They would never be this
young, this pure, or this dedicated to one another again.

It had been my privilege to watch them invent and reinvent
themselves day after day. Life had battered them, hammering
their hearts and spirits, like it does all kids. Most of these boys
had difficult lives, as difficult as Carter's had been in Texas.
Some had been physically assaulted, emotionally terrified, or
both. But, it hadn't put them down. It had made them tougher.
Tempered by disappointment, they were more determined not
to accept defeat or to be denied. They were good kids filled
with resolve and collective energy that now began to feed them
and renew them.

They encouraged Carter and watched Shaun out at second,
dancing off the bag and chattering like a monkey at the Kalamazoo pitcher.

Suddenly the Furies took hold of the team. Their commitment
and intensity became a tidal surge of focused madness explod-
ing from the confines of the dugout and sweeping them all into
a frenzy—a demand to reorder this moment in time and to
change what had already seemed to be destiny. They had taken
command and were setting a new course. They had come to
play and to win, nothing short of that would suffice. They were
riding the whirlwind.

The energy blew through me as I stood near them, and a
Chinook of adrenaline churned my stomach. I nearly vomited.
Feeling the energy watching the kids coalesce at such a basic
level was exhilarating, but also frightening, because I knew it

could not last—that primal bond of undeniable intent, bright and clear and doubtless.

Aware of how little I could do for them in their "real" lives, I felt small and weak and deeply flawed. They were kids, I liked them, and I could not stand to see them hurt. I had watched these boys grow. I had coached midget League, Little League, Pony League, Babe Ruth, and finally Connie Mack. But, it was quite possible that I would hurt them more than anybody, by letting them believe in something that I was no longer sure I believed in myself.

My broken soul had long ago gotten too many wrong answers to my questions of faith and belief in sports. I began hedging and refused to put all my hopes and love and commitment into the purity of the game. I held out, pulled back, saving a bit of myself, just in case. But I told the kids to believe and give everything they had. I let them live on hope and told white lies. I promised that their sacrifice would be rewarded, their dedication repaid in kind, and their discipline would make them honest men.

They were real. I was fake. I neatly rationalized my decision to spend so much time with Carter and his teammates as the caring, concerned, and selfless adult and parent. But, I knew deep down my real reason was selfish—I wanted the time with Carter. The terrors of divorce had slammed home the reality that the time Carter and I had together was rapidly running out. I was clawing for every second, every minute to be with him, holding on to each moment until it was ripped away.

Just as I had bumbled selfishly through those past summer baseball seasons, enjoying every precious second, I had planned to fool my way through this one. But instead I had brought Carter and his team to this awful moment—this "playoff game."

Now, Carter was out there all alone at the plate, one strike away from disaster. In my selfish vanity to be the best father ever, to justify myself as a volunteer coach, I had put Carter in harm's way.

I had forgotten the first rule of being a father and a coach.

None of this was about me; it was about the players, it was about Carter.

Carter was not scared. Carter was exactly where he wanted to be—at the plate and standing tall, facing down KTOO's pitcher. He stood there defiantly and took on Greg Grosvenor head to head. If Grosvenor wanted Carter down, he was going to have to put him down. Carter had the game and the season riding on his bat. Every other kid on the team was out there with him.

He was savoring this instant that had so much potential for joy or disaster, this instant that he knew would never come again. Carter had spent the last ten years preparing for it and he wouldn't have had it any other way. A dance on the high wire. Nerves cold. Heart hot. Spirit soaring. Mind converging. Body coiled. Waiting. Waiting. Waiting.

The sounds from our dugout were unintelligible ... almost animal.

Shaun was extending his lead and talking to Grosvenor, who was beginning his stretch. The second baseman took a couple of steps toward the bag, trying to pull Shaun back.

Greg Grosvenor began his stretch.

Time stood still.

6 ◇ Gunmen

THE STUFF OF MAJOR nightmares and accidental homicides, two gunmen showed up at our house the week after my wife had disappeared. When I saw the men wearing jeans and western shirts with guns on their hips, I told Carter and Crystal, his playmate, to get into the bathtub in the back bathroom.

In the years I had lived in Texas, I had many guns pulled on me and had been shot at several times. Whether or not I deserved it was a separate question. Either way, I took armed men seriously.

After checking their badges and IDs while standing in my open doorway, blocking access to the house, I tried to comprehend the mass of papers the two gunslingers handed me. The filing for divorce was pretty clear. The woman wanted out of the fourteen years of marriage that she considered a living hell. It was the other two documents I could not digest.

The first was my wife's affidavit swearing she had fled for her life wearing only the clothes on her back. She failed to mention all the cash, deeds, contracts, bank accounts, eleven hundred ounces of silver bars, and two hundred ounces of gold coins. Now, after having safely stashed the swag, she was back for Carter and the house by swearing I was going to murder him. The second document was an accompanying writ of attachment for "the body of Carter Davis Gent."

"Who are you guys, again?" I asked. I knew all the lawmen in Hays County where we lived.

"Travis County deputies," the closer one answered. The other deputy was standing idly by picking his nose. "We are here to pick up the boy."

Pick up the boy? I froze for a long moment, my mind spinning. "Whaddaya mean? Where are you taking him?" I managed to say.

"To his mother."

"Where is she?"

"We don't have to tell you that. Just get the boy."

"I don't think I'll be able to do that until I see somebody I know," I said. "I just can't hand over my kid to strangers."

"We are deputies," the first one said, showing me his ID again and pointing at the papers I was holding. "Those are court orders."

"I'm sorry, anybody can get a deputy's badge in Texas," I said. "And Judge Ramsey's signature wouldn't have gotten you up the drive if I had seen you coming. Until I see somebody I trust, my six-year-old stays here."

"Then, we will just have to take him."

"I don't think you oughta try that." I had been resting my right hand on my hip. I slid it slowly toward the fourteen-shot

Smith & Wesson nine-millimeter automatic jammed in my belt at the small of my back. "That would be a bigger mistake than staking your life on Charlie Ramsey's signature."

For the first time the deputies sensed trouble. They were three steps behind the game. Deadly tension filled the air. It was not a good feeling. But I was in and could see no way out short of giving Carter to two total strangers—and that was just never gonna happen.

Panicked, I waited on the deputies' next move. My stomach turned flops with fear. If they tried to go over me for Carter, what would I do? If they threatened deadly force, could I really kill them? We seemed to be heading toward disaster. And one thing was absolutely certain: I was not going to hand Carter over to two armed strangers at dusk on a Friday night without the most god-awful fight—and I had been in some god-awful fights.

Terrible decisions were going through all of our minds, when miraculously Jimmy Whitten, a Hays County deputy, roared up my driveway in his patrol car. Jimmy had heard these two deputies radio back to the Travis County sheriff in Austin when they reached my house. He knew my wife had vanished a week earlier because he and Sonny Gold, the local justice of the peace, had been trying to find her for the past several days. He interceded for me with the deputies and promised he would go with Carter and make certain that he was taken to his mother.

"I don't want to go, Dad," Carter said. Carter was crying. Crystal was crying too.

"Jimmy is gonna take you to see your mom," I said. "You want to see your mom, don't you?"

"Yeah, but I'm scared."

"You know Jimmy, Carter." I waved Deputy Whitten into the back bedroom where I was packing Carter's little suitcase.

"Hi, Carter," Whitten said. "Do you want to go with me to see your mom?"

Carter looked from Jimmy to me back to Jimmy and back to me. He was scared and confused. So was I.

"What should I do, Dad?"

"Go with Jimmy. He'll take you to see your mom. I will see you in a few days."

"Okay, I'll go."

I handed Jimmy Carter's suitcase and watched them leave the house. As he walked out the door, Carter's head just came up to the Pachmyar grip of the Travis deputy's holstered pistol.

Jimmy was back in ten minutes.

"Your wife was in a limo in the Wimberley Bank lot with her lawyer." Jimmy was angry. "She said you were going to kill her."

"Well, somebody nearly got killed here. I couldn't think what to do." I exhaled and began to shake. "I wasn't letting them take him . . . beyond that I had no plans."

"Beyond that, you had no future." Jimmy frowned and watched me. "A killing would have simplified the divorce for your wife. You're either dead or in jail."

It was a scarey thought. Had it been planned?

I didn't see Carter or talk to him again for three weeks. It seemed like three years. Finally, the temporary orders came down: In return for my giving Carter's mother possession of the house, the judge portioned Carter out to me for a generous four days a month.

When I first went to pick him up, I was shocked by the dark blue circles under his eyes. He looked sick. Only four days a month of visitation was unbearable for us and I phoned and asked his mother for more time. She refused.

"Remember," Tom Keating told me over the phone from his home near Oakland, "to her Carter is just a bargaining chip. She knows Carter is the one way she can hurt you." I called ex-U of M and Oakland Raider star Keating constantly for advice throughout the ensuing custody fight. Twice he and his family drove all the way to Texas to support Carter and me when the battles got particularly ugly.

But first, to get more time with Carter, I started skating on the thin ice of civil disobedience. I met him for lunch at the elementary school, he slipped up to a neighbor's house for games of catch, and I went to the baseball field to watch Carter's Tee Ball team practice and had gladly agreed to his coaches' request to help with the team. Neither judges nor jail were going to keep us apart forever.

Carter had been taken away by gunmen and it had left scars. I told him I would get to him every chance I had. It was the deal I had to keep. I swore to him I would always be there. I had no idea how I would keep the promise; I just knew I had to keep it.

So Carter and I grabbed the moments and minutes when we could. It became the game we played. They were playing for money. We were playing for time.

7 ◇ July 23, 1992—The Playoff Game

"COME ON, CARTER," Chris Christian yelled. "Rope that ball."

Most of the kids that made up this team had known each other since October 1985, when I brought Carter back to go to Bangor elementary school. He was in the fourth grade.

When he was growing up in Bangor, Carter ran around with Ben and Eric Finch, Christ Christian, Shaun Eisner, and Steve Leonard. These kids had been his friends for years, playing sandlot baseball and pickup basketball together. Mike Wisser and Mike Wisniewski moved to Bangor around the time Carter got into high school. At one time or another, I had coached them all in summer baseball.

It seemed like the only time my life was half organized were those summers that I coached, when I had to be there for games and practices. There was nothing to compare with watching these kids amaze themselves with their developing skills. Before they were done, they would amaze me.

The only way to keep away old age was to hang around kids. Kids make you feel young, they make you act young. If you don't keep up with them, they leave you behind. Carter and his teammates kept me young in a world that had already grown old twice on me. I knew the third time would be for real: I would be old.

At twenty-seven years old, I had squandered my health in the National Football League. I had rebuilt my life writing books and movies by the time I was thirty-seven. I lost it all again in the bitter divorce that started when I was forty. The recovery from the divorce would take the rest of the time I had with Carter and I was determined not to waste any of it.

Carter's rapid athletic improvement in spite of the turmoil that filled his life taught him that he could succeed, that things would improve through practice, discipline, dedication, and commitment to his friends and teammates and to a purpose. I can still see the first looks of amazement on Carter's face when he was suddenly confronted by the reality of a minor success. He could hit the ball. He could make the catch. He could throw strikes. These simple victories when he desperately needed to believe in himself were invaluable. He learned he could play the game. By becoming a player, he had rediscovered a belief in himself.

Baseball undid a lot of damage. It is important for a coach to remember he may well be the first and only surrogate parent a child has. A coach can do much good; he can also inflict much harm. A coach can hold the spirit and soul of a young athlete in his hands, for good or ill. Being a coach is a great responsibility and a great honor. But, at this particular moment of our "playoff game" against Kalamazoo Too, it was causing me great stress.

The count on Carter was 0–2. We trailed, 4–3. Carter had shortened his stance, choked up on the bat, and was protecting the plate.

Stretching and checking Shaun at second, Grosvenor delivered his next pitch up and inside. Carter fell back. I winced and ducked reflexively. The fastball blew by head high.

The Bangor players started on Grosvenor.

"Take that cheese back to Kalamazoo, meat," Chris Christian yelled.

"Throw that junk at me," Mike Wisniewski hollered, "I'll take your ass downtown, Grosvenor."

He was throwing all fastballs—I was sure the next pitch was going to kill Carter and it would be all my fault.

"Come in closer," Jeff Tennis, the KTOO coach, yelled to his outfield. "This guy isn't a power hitter."

The Kalamazoo Too outfielders cheated up even closer. The count was now 1–2. Shaun was still at second ... the tying run. There was still one out.

"That's a boy, Greg," the KTOO players chattered. "Don't let him dig in. He's no hitter. No stick up there."

Carter took a couple of deep breaths, adjusted his batting gloves, looked out at the mound, then stepped back into the box.

My stomach turned over and an icy hand reached into my chest, grabbed my heart, and stopped it cold. I couldn't breathe. Good God. How did I get Carter in this mess?

Both dugouts were in a frenzy. The Bangor players were harassing Grosvenor on the mound and encouraging Carter at the plate. The KTOO players were cheering Grosvenor and heckling Carter.

Carter stepped away from the box and bent over. He was trying to relax and concentrate. He had already ordered me not to yell encouragement from the dugout. "Your voice bugs me," he had said to me. "It doesn't bother me when the other guys are yelling. It's just ... there's something about your voice. I don't know. It ... it ... it *bugs me!*"

"And"—he had been merciless—"quit yelling at me to keep my elbow up ... always yelling 'elbow!' You're driving me nuts."

Carter stretched and gathered himself, ready to approach the plate. Today was a test of his stamina. It had been a long day. He studied the field. Shaun Eisner, the tying run, was beginning to look like a permanent fixture on second base.

Relaxed and confident, Carter moved back into the box. Grosvenor stepped on the rubber. I was sick with fear.

Shaun took a long lead from second. He was determined to score on a single. Shaun was like that. He gambled and played hard. During the summer he had come through with some big plays along with a couple of big mistakes.

Grosvenor stretched, and suddenly the second baseman broke for the bag. A pickoff play! They had caught Shaun leaning toward third. He turned and scrambled back, diving for the bag.

"Get back! Get back!" everybody was yelling at Eisner. "Goddamnit, Shaun . . . you idiot!"

Grosvenor whirled and threw. The second baseman was there. They were sure they had Shaun cold as he went in headfirst, one hand reaching for the bag. The throw was slightly high and the second baseman missed the tag as Shaun twisted and slid away from his glove. Safe!

The KTOO players howled. The Bangor players gasped, then sighed. My knees gave out and I had to go sit down. The dugout had started to spin.

"Jesus! Shaun!" Carter said, out of the box again, collecting himself again.

Shaun was up and dusted himself off. Time was back in. The pitcher had the ball and Carter was back in the box waiting. Grosvenor stretched. He grunted loud as he came down off the mound, slinging a bullet. Jesus! He was a big guy!

Carter stepped forward, then checked his swing and watched the ball go by. Low and outside. The count was 2–2.

What was Carter thinking up there? What kind of pitch was he expecting? Advantage was slowly turning back in his direction. Grosvenor respected Carter as a hitter and had to stay on top with this next pitch. He did not want to give Carter a full count. Carter was a smart batter.

Grosvenor stretched and checked Shaun who simply refused to be scared into staying closer to second. Shaun danced and chattered.

Meanwhile, keeping his compact stance, Carter quickly moved up in the box. If Grosvenor threw a breaking ball, Carter wanted to get on it before it broke very far. But Grosvenor's fastball would be on him like lightning.

It was a big gamble. But Carter had been studying Grosvenor the whole season. He knew he would throw a curve in this situation. Grosvenor turned back and delivered the curveball, directly toward the middle of the plate. The ball would break down and away from Carter.

The strategy of the pitch was good had Carter been back in the box. If Carter did not swing, the ball would catch the outside corner, a called third strike. If Carter did swing, the ball would break away from him and he would go down swinging—or he might fight off the pitch with a foul tip.

The ball did exactly what Grosvenor wanted, headed for the middle, soon to start to hook and drop away. It looked like the perfect tactical pitch.

Except ... Carter had bet on the curve. Quickly picking up the ball's rotation, he stepped forward and started his sweet swing. His bat had good speed, connecting solid. He rolled his wrists over and drove a line shot over the outfielder's head into deep center.

Shaun scored the tying run and the Bangor players went nuts as Carter went into second standing up.

Carter's double started a three-run rally that got us the win, and the seed, for the 1992 AABC Connie Mack State District Tournament. Carter had done it, just as he knew he would and I feared he wouldn't.

I sat in the dugout and watched the Bangor kids hug and jump all over one another. Above it all I could hear Carter's laugh. I wished the moment would never end. I wished he could go back and play the whole game over again.

Carter's wry sense of humor and infectious laugh had saved my sanity and my life on more than one occasion. He had done it again and hearing his laughter now made all the misery we had ever endured worthwhile.

Little Bangor had beaten Kalamazoo Too and had taken KTOO's perennial place in the Kalamazoo AABC Connie Mack State District Tournament. Mike Hinga and the Maroons organization would never forgive us or forget the shame: Bangor's eight-dollar players beating his highly skilled, well-coached three-hundred-dollar KTOO all-stars. Even though all the rain had fallen the night before in Bangor, Kalamazoo was Mudville that July evening.

8 ◇ A Walk in the Past

"I'M BORED," CARTER SAID, walking around my office.

"Let's take a walk and settle down," I suggested.

A walk would do me good. The 1993 schedule was printed out and ready to give to my players. It was going to be our last summer in Connie Mack.

Carter and I walked to Distefano's Amoco and were looking at the Bangor Lumber Company across Monroe Street. I could remember when the huge fruit orchards literally ran up to within a block of downtown.

"Bangor is sure going downhill," I said. "All the jobs went south. And they ain't coming back."

We walked through the drive of Distefano's Amoco station and turned west at the blinking light and headed toward the two blocks of downtown. "It sure had a lot more going on downtown," I added.

We then stood directly across from Harding's Market on Monroe Street. Harding's was the last grocery store in town and a large part of its business was food stamps. Once there had been five grocers. They had all accepted phone orders and delivered.

"That's where you played football and baseball, right?" Carter pointed to the old combination field behind Harding's Market.

"Yep. It sure isn't as fancy as the football/track stadium and ball diamonds you've got over by the new school," I said. "But, we got by and won championships in everything but track."

"I know, Dad. You mentioned it before."

"Really?"

"Yeah, I think you told me the moment I was born."

"But, just that once?"

"And now. That makes two. So back off." He grimaced and punched my shoulder.

"Looking to get whipped?" I put my hands up.

"You steppin' up on me?" He danced around, throwing open-handed punches against my shoulders and chest. "You want some of this? We can throw down right here. Come on, sucker."

"Try it and I'll hit you so hard Hollywood will option the rights to your memoirs of the trip."

"What?" Carter laughed and backed away. I began walking again and he waited for me on the sidewalk, falling in step when I reached him.

"So, Daddy," he mocked. "Tell me more. Puuleeeze."

"All right, pay attention because I will have this on the mid-term. Lemme see." I sighed long and loud. "Okay, there were two dairies in Bangor that processed and delivered milk and dairy products right to our door every morning."

We passed the twenty-four-hour self-service gas station and mini-mart, the only change, besides the video store, that I found useful in Bangor. When I was a kid the town was shut up tight by 6:00 P.M. and radio was our only home entertainment.

I pointed across the street to the dentist's office. "Used to be a factory there that built motor scooters," I said. "Next to it was a movie theater, a drugstore, a restaurant, a hobby shop, and an appliance store run by the Indiana Michigan Utility Company."

Carter looked at the decimated block and tried to imagine all the stores and people and bustle that was long gone. The block was now dominated by Lander's Hardware and a liquor store/

restaurant recently purchased by a retired cop from Chicago who drove an Excalibur.

Up a block the C & O railroad tracks that came around the south end of Lake Michigan from Chicago bisected the two blocks of downtown Bangor.

"On both sides of the blocks going west across the railroad tracks to the town hall was the major retail part of town."

I began pointing out buildings as we passed them.

"This was an IGA grocery store. Chris Christian's uncle Floyd worked there as a carryout boy. The A&P was here. Miller's Hardware was in one of these buildings ... then the Smoke Shop was here next to the Bangor Hotel ..."

"Bangor had a hotel?" Carter was amazed. "People stayed in the Bangor Hotel?"

"I used to see people sitting in the lobby every day as I walked by," I replied. "Krenn's Men's Clothing was here ... white bucks, pink and black shirts, and high-style sweaters."

We walked past the video store.

"From here to the railroad tracks was Moskowitz Five and Dime filled with doodads made in Japan." I stopped in front of a big abandoned building, leaning against the big windows next to the FOR RENT sign and peered inside. "Cheapest stuff you could buy was made in Japan. I used to spend hours wandering around in this store. Your uncle Charlie's first job was here. He made sixty cents an hour and they worked his butt off."

"Sixty cents an hour? That's not even five dollars a day." Carter squinted through the dusty windows.

"Things didn't cost much then," I said. "Gas was twenty-five cents a gallon. An RC Cola was a nickel. Times have changed."

"I've noticed. RCs cost a buck now." Carter paused to look up and down the street. "All that stuff was in this one block?"

I nodded. "Plus there were offices for lawyers, doctors, and dentists in the second stories, even some apartments."

"What was that big empty building we passed a block back?"

"Standard Coil Company, first," I said. "Then, later it was

Adams Electronics. They employed three hundred people and got started in the late forties supplying the radio and television industry in Chicago."

I stopped and turned back to look at the abandoned plant. My parents had known the executives and plant workers. Their kids had grown up in Bangor or South Haven and I knew all of them.

"In a town of two thousand people, three hundred jobs were a lot," I said to Carter. "Tony Eicas was plant manager there."

"That's where Tony Eicas worked? What happened?"

"While we were living in Wimberley, they sold out to Tracor, a big Austin electronics company and defense contractor," I explained. "Tracor immediately shut the plant down as a tax write-off. Three hundred jobs in the toilet. Really hurt Bangor."

"They bought it to close it down?" Carter asked. "That is tight. Couldn't anybody do anything?"

"Strange you should ask." I chewed on my lip. "I ran into Tracor's CEO at a party at Liz Carpenter's in Austin and threatened to spread him on the walls like onion dip. As far as I know, that was all the negative reaction he got from Bangor."

"Was Mom with you?" Carter looked at me.

"Right beside me. I was shaking hands with the guy and just starting squeezing hard, telling him I was gonna bounce him off the walls. I just get warm all over when I think about it."

"Jesus, Dad, I can't believe you." Carter stared at me. "What happened?"

"He just kept grinning this lopsided grin as the tips of his fingers turned white and his knuckles ground. Then, he began to bend at the knees," I continued. "Your mom was tugging on my arm, telling me to turn him loose. She was pissed."

Reciting the story there reminded me how much of Bangor's once-bright future had been sold out by people who never even set foot in the town.

I remembered what Bangor had once been in the early fifties. Standard Coil had just built its new plant right downtown on Monroe Street. DuWel Metal had its new casting plant north of

town on the Black River and often ran three shifts keeping up
with orders from the Big Three in Detroit.

"Was the Bangor Grain Elevator and Fruit Exchange always
there by the railroad tracks?" Carter pointed across the street,
drawing me back.

"It was one of about six that lined the tracks clear back behind
the old athletic field to the Black River trestle."

"I remember some of those old buildings. When we first moved
back here. Ben and Eric Finch and I climbed all through the
tumbledown old warehouses." Carter paused, his brow fur-
rowed. "The police would chase us off."

"Good God, Carter!" I just shook my head. "Those buildings
were all condemned and full of toxic and explosive chemicals."

"Ben fell through the floor of one of them. But they tore 'em
down before we could explore them all." Carter smiled his
wicked smile. "Dad, if you had any idea the stuff we did when
you weren't around."

"Please, spare me. It's why I coached baseball." I held up my
hands. "I don't want to know that if I had only scheduled more
games you wouldn't have grown that second head when you
turned twenty-one."

"Remember last summer when Nuke worked at the pickle
factory?" Carter laughed. "He fell into the giant pickle vat and
came over to the house stinking and soaking wet? Remember?"

"How could I forget?"

We both laughed hard at the recollection of an embarrassed
Mike Wisniewski walking through the front door, drenched in
pickle brine, looking like a drowned rat with his wry, puppy dog
smile accenting his full cheeks, flushed red.

"You know"—I caught my breath—"Bangor used to ship box-
cars full of farm produce and fruit to Chicago for years and
years. There were lots of profitable family farms here."

We studied the weed-covered foundations of the old fruit warehouses and farm supply stores, the abandoned boxcar siding.

"Most of the farms have gone bust and the land bought up

by Chicago real estate lawyers. Your great-grandfather had a hundred and twenty acres of apples, peaches, pears, cherries, plums, and vineyards up by . . ."

"You've shown me where it was, Dad." Carter stopped me. "Every time we go to Breedsville you show me where the farm was and the forty acres where Grandpa planted all the pine trees."

"I lost the pine trees in the divorce," I said.

Carter ignored the remark. He didn't want to discuss the divorce or the loss of trees. I didn't either, really. It was just that I kept trying to get somebody to forgive me.

My father had planted thousands of trees as seedlings during the Depression and then hand-cultivated them until they took root and grew into a dense forest of evergreen. It had been backbreaking work. But, it was as close to a religion as my father ever got. Over the years, economics had forced him to sell off all but the forty acres. His pride and joy, they were a wonderland of every species of pine that grew in Michigan. Carter's grandfather had loved and cared for the forty acres for almost five decades before signing them over to me and my wife when Carter was born. First he extracted the promise that they would never be sold.

I lost the land in the property settlement the year Carter's grandfather died. I could never get up the nerve to tell him. But I think he knew.

"Across the track up the next block was a butcher shop, the pool hall"—I changed the subject—"Swantra's Drug—"

"Swantra's is still there," Carter interrupted.

"Same place but without the big soda fountain, jukebox, and booths. It was a big hangout after school. Next door was a furniture store, then the Copper Kettle which was another restaurant."

"How many restaurants did you have?" Carter was amazed.

"Five or six, I think." I frowned.

"Bangor had five or six restaurants?" Carter stared at me.

"Hey, fella, we had six full-service gas stations. Ralph Lowder's Cities Service was over there. The Sinclair station was up the block. Gulf was east of town. Angelo had Standard Oil then . . . and . . . ah . . .''

"Yeah," Carter said, smirking at me. "What else?"

"There were others, like Texaco," I added. "You could always get a job pumping gas, checking oil, and washing cars.

"The old bank was torn down." I pointed across the street. "The new one is where Charlie Cross, the bank president, had his house. In 1940, Charlie loaned your grandpa two thousand dollars to buy the house you're living in."

"Two thousand?" Carter studied the new bank and tried to imagine what Bangor looked like in 1940. "That's fresh."

"Ely Hardware is still in the same place it's always been." I pointed down the block. "There was another grocery store just past Ely's and two funeral homes on the corners across from the Town Hall. Death has always been good business in Bangor."

I studied the street and tried to remember back forty-plus years.

"Down another couple blocks was a Nash dealership, a Chrysler Plymouth dealer—the DeSoto sign is still on the building." I pointed west toward South Haven. "Irv's Place was farther out near the edge of town."

"What about back there by the new post office?" Carter asked, pointing north toward the abandoned railroad depot.

"There was another lumberyard, a plumbing supply store, and Ed's Cab which was also a restaurant as well as a taxi service."

"Bangor had a taxi cab company? That is too diggity." Carter laughed. "Did a lot of people come in by train?"

"Especially in the summer," I told Carter. "People could take the train to Chicago in the morning and return that night. Your grandpa worked on the railway mail. He loved the trains."

"I wouldn't mind a job traveling on a train like that," Carter said. "A lot better than working in a store."

"The depot would be jammed with people on weekends," I said. "Porters stacking luggage on big green wagons, mail clerks loading mailbags. The conductor standing on the red Streator Brick, checking his watch, ready to signal the engineer."

"Why were all the people coming to Bangor?"

"Besides on Lake Michigan, people had summer cottages on all the little lakes around here," I explained. "South Haven was a big summer resort for Jewish families." I was searching for the way to explain a way of life long gone. "It looked like . . . like . . ."

"Like that place in *Dirty Dancing*?" Carter brightened up. Suddenly, he could see it. "That must have been weird."

"It was also really exciting," I said. "From the Fourth of July to Labor Day all these new people and this whole different style of life ten miles away in South Haven."

"Did you ride on the train with Grandpa?"

"Both your uncles and I each got to ride in the mail car once, all the way to Chicago and back. It was our rite of passage into your grandpa's world of the railroads and life in the fifties."

"Was it fun?"

"Being a kid in a Chicago train depot at rush hour in the early fifties was amazing," I said. "Anything was possible in America and Bangor was connected by steel rails. It was America and we were a part of it."

"It's hard to imagine all that." Carter looked up and down the blocks and over at the abandoned depot and boxcar siding.

"We had just won World War Two. We were still the good guys," I said to Carter. "We were the most powerful nation in history and things would just get better."

I stopped talking and looked around. I had not succeeded in transporting myself back in time. I was not a seven-year-old with his future ahead and shining bright. I was a fifty-one-year-old man, trying to explain a long-lost past filled with missed chances, wasted opportunity, and bad memories. Bangor and I were the same. Our best years were behind us and the future looked bleak and short. We were trapped like bugs in amber between the dying American Dream and the Emerging New World Order.

"What else was here?" Carter asked.

I looked at Carter. It was strange telling him about these things. So much I had forgotten. So much that seemed unreal.

"At Irv's Place nobody ever heard of cholesterol," I prattled on. "We got huge, greasy, twenty-five-cent hamburgers with fries, ten-cent cokes, a jukebox full of Elvis, Buddy Holly, and the Everly Brothers."

"It's hard to see it." Carter studied the abandoned and run-down buildings as if all these things might reappear if we talked long enough. "What? Sort of like *Happy Days?*"

"Not exactly. The Fonz woulda got his ass stomped by every farm kid who came to Bangor High when it was consolidated. The cars were the same nosed and decked, stroked and bored, Detroit iron."

"Like low riders?" Carter saw a lot of low riders on MTV and Black Entertainment Network videos.

"Yeah, except without the Uzis and Mac-10s," I said.

"What happened to Irv's Place?" Carter asked.

"They tore it down and built a car wash," I said.

"It figures." Carter frowned. "Let's head back. Your legs must be getting sore."

They were. We walked back and turned south on Railroad Street and began working our way to my office. We passed near the free clinic for indigents and migrants and the building where once a week they lined up for free government cheese.

"Does it seem like it all went by real fast?" Carter asked, kicking a stone down the street.

"Sometimes it seems like it went by so fast that it never even happened." I turned to cross the tracks.

Carter and I didn't talk on the walk back to the office.

Carter had his mind on the Kalamazoo Maroons and the coming summer baseball season.

I was back inside Irv's Place with the flattops and the DAs, the poodle skirts and the penny loafers, the motorcycle boots and leather jackets with multidirectional zippers, and the Jack Purcell basketball shoes.

9 ◇ Irv's Place

IRV'S PLACE WAS WHERE the high school kids hung out after football and basketball games, sock hops, Sadie Hawkins dances, the Snowball, Homecoming, and the Junior-Senior Hunt. Kids came after school and on Saturday night dates.

The little side road that angled off of M–43 west of town at Irv's Place and then rejoined the highway just east of Thomas' Slaughter House was the west end turnaround on the main drag that ran east and west down Monroe Street. The east end turnaround was at the angled juncture of M–43 and Arlington Street.

The whole main drag run was a little under a mile and on weekend nights in the summer was like a black river filled with shiny, shimmering, flashing, jumping, and wiggling metal fish. They were gorgeous machines, muscle cars, fuel-injected, dual fours, three twos, big blocks, convertibles, hardtops, stock or custom. The power of a generation paraded up and down Monroe Street in the best cars Detroit would make for the next thirty years. Detroit, like Bangor, was reaching a turning point. But, neither town knew it yet.

Bangor flourished. Nobody got shot on Saturday night. People never locked their doors. During summer, most slept with their windows and doors open. The screens kept out the mosquitoes and conversations drifted from one house to another. Nobody had air-conditioning.

The summer days and nights were cool because the whole town was shaded by huge American elms. Neighbors sat out on their porches after dinner and visited with their friends walking by.

Later at night, my dad would sit with me and point out the constellations—I wanted to be an astronomer or an archaeologist.

By my senior year Bangor High School's football and basketball programs were dominant statewide and in the Kalamazoo Valley Association (KVA), a conference of other teams with statewide reputations. A small class C school, we only had four men's interscholastic sports and no women's sports. Boys played ball. Girls were cheerleaders, pom-pom girls, or in the band. Bangor High School's enrollment was so small that lots of kids had to play all four sports just for there to be enough bodies. Baseball games and track meets could not be scheduled on the same day because two thirds of the baseball team ran track.

As the middle son in our family, I had the great good fortune to play high school sports with both of my brothers. In 1957 we won, 7–6, against our arch rival Paw Paw in our first KVA Football Championship. The one-point difference was the extra point kicked by my brother Charlie. The only extra point he ever attempted in a game in his entire football career and he made it.

In three years we lost only two games and won KVA and state titles. As a senior in 1959–1960, I played the four sports with my younger brother, Jamie. Again we won KVA and state titles. Jamie was a fourteen-year-old sophomore first-string forward on our 1960 state championship basketball team.

We didn't play sports in those days. We lived them. For everything there was a season and we lived that season. A time for football. A time for basketball. And a time that had to be split for baseball and track. What our time playing sports at Bangor High School gave us was the exultation of our youth. We succeeded much more than we failed. I, for one, have done nothing that well since, or enjoyed anything as much as then ... when I was young.

The seasons of youth, when we played as only young men can, will carry me with grace until it is the time to die. It took me years to recapture that state of grace I had learned on the fields of my youth: how to live and die with style and poise. For a long time, I lived in fear that I had lost it all. It was by watching Carter struggle with the same monsters in life that I realized the lessons never left me. Those victories could never be taken away by others or diminished by age and infirmity. We had lived as champions. We will die champions.

In the fifties and sixties, Bangor had prospered. The school system flourished. The athletic programs were in ascendancy.

All that was gone now. The stores, the car dealers, John Deere and International Harvester, the lumberyards, the factories, the dairies, the fruit exchanges, Irv's place, Moskowitz Five and Ten, Krenn's Men's Clothing, DuWel Metal, Bangor Plastics, Standard Coil, the jobs, and the dreams.

Gone.

In Bangor, Dutch elm disease killed all the American elms and the town grew progressively hotter each summer.

Now, there was one drugstore and no soda fountains, two video shops, a liquor store, a couple of fast-food restaurants, a magic shop, and a tanning salon. The bank was still there, but nobody was borrowing much money and nobody seemed too anxious to loan. You've got to have a dream before you can finance it. You've got to have hope before you nail yourself down to paying back with interest.

The passenger train to Chicago cut its service to three days a week.

Now, the biggest payroll in town was the Bangor public school system which functioned like a branch of a multinational corporation. The kids were just products to be punched out and shipped off fast—stamped "some assembly required." School administrators passed through like young GM executives on the fast track to Detroit. Bangor's school system was sick—infected by a gatepost stupid school board; grasping, ambitious administrators; and teachers and coaches with no investment of time or emotion in the kids or town.

The quality of education and athletics at Bangor High School began its inexorable slide into mediocrity in the seventies. The superintendent and school board who had built the new schools and athletic plants were victims of slanderous attacks by the coterie of a fired coach. The superintendent resigned and the school board was recalled. After that disaster, the winning sports program and the school's educational quality were history.

The new football stadium–track rivaled those of many small colleges. The new basketball arena was top-notch and often hosted district and regional tournaments because of its quality and seating capacity. The track with its expensive artificial surface hosted the State Class C Track Meet. But, this top-of-the-line, state-of-the-art plant was soon inhabited by mediocre programs.

The talent pool of kids seemed larger than ever. Yet, despite the quality of the facilities and players, the basketball team never returned to the state finals. The football team was no longer a feared statewide power. Carter's coaches watched television for their game plans and theories. Damage was done.

10 ◇ The Texas Diaries—1983

When the armies are mobilized and the forces joined, the one who is sorry over the fact will win.

—LAO-TZU

THE FEBRUARY 1983 TEMPORARY ORDERS allowing me to see Carter only four days a month were too ruthless to be endured. Carter could not stand living with his mother and seeing him only two weekends a month was killing me. We had been together nearly every day since I had watched him being born in the hospital in Kalamazoo.

"Mom is mean to me and there are all these people around I don't know," Carter told me. "She told me she is going to marry some guy and he is going to be my new dad. I told her I missed you and she said she would get me a puppy . . . isn't that strange?"

"Take her up on the puppy," I said. "You might as well get another pet out of this mess."

Carter's mother brought home a miniature poodle puppy that Carter named Rosie.

"Ask Mom if you can be my baby-sitter," Carter insisted the next time I saw him. He was angry. "She's a greedy, lying bitch."

"Don't call her names," I said. It was obvious that our divorce was dinner table conversation throughout Wimberley and his schoolmates were bringing tales from home to the playground. I didn't even want to think what people were calling me. Worried, I called her the same night.

"Let me baby-sit Carter," I said. "He wants it. You'd have more freedom . . ."

"No, I already have a baby-sitter. You stay away from him," she replied.

"But, I'd do it anytime, at a moment's notice. Carter wants—"

"It doesn't matter what he wants," she said, and hung up on me.

"Your mom has another baby-sitter," I told Carter when I saw him next.

Tears welled up in his eyes, which were surrounded by blue-black circles that stood out in stark contrast to his pale white skin. He looked and moved like a little old man. "Mom doesn't know anything," he said, staring out the window of the yellow Plymouth Duster I had borrowed from my friend Sonny Gold. "You know I heard about this little boy whose mom didn't like him and he hanged himself in the barn."

"Carter!" I pulled off the road and studied Carter's face. "Nothing has happened that can't be fixed, and, as terrible as we feel right now, we might feel great tomorrow."

"Mom tells people she wishes you were dead."

"I can't help that and neither can you," I said. Carter didn't seem suicidal and this was the first time he had ever mentioned it.

With the fingers of both hands, I began kneading the ever-present knots in his neck and shoulder muscles. "Now listen to me. At one time or another, everybody thinks about killing himself. But, actually trying to kill yourself is wrong. What would your sister, Holly, do? What would I do?"

"This little boy did it and his mom was sorry about the way she treated him." Carter looked right at me. "She was always lying to him and he just hangded himself in the barn."

"Carter, promise me that if you are ever as unhappy as that little boy, you will call me and talk about it," I said. "This is one of those things you should always put off until tomorrow. Promise me?"

"Okay," he said, and stood in the passenger seat and walked over to put his left arm around my neck. "I promise."

"If you can't find me," I pressed, "promise you will call Sonny Gold or Laurel before you do anything."

"All right." He was fidgeting, anxious that we get moving. Suicide seemed the furthest thing from his mind. "I promise."

"Call me at night," Carter said next. "You can tell me a bed-time story over the phone." He was scared and could not sleep.

So I called and told him bedtime stories. His favorite story was about his Tee Ball team winning the world championship against the Japanese champions in the Astrodome in front of thousands in attendance and billions on television. Carter would make all the great defensive plays and always hit the game-winning grand slam home run.

"Tell me the part again," he would interrupt, "where I jump twenty feet in the air to make the catch."

And I would, often stretching the story out for a couple of hours before he would finally fall asleep. I had to stay on the phone so he did not wake up and find I had hung up. Sometimes, I waited another hour, listening to the sound of his breathing, until his mother came into the room and hung up the phone.

Carter was miserable living with his mother. He constantly nagged her to let him come and live with me at Sonny and Laurel Gold's house, where I had taken up residence. Suddenly, on April 20, 1983, Carter's mother granted him his wish to stay with me. In return, I promised to bring him to see her every day after school. It was as close to a perfect arrangement as we could hope for.

"Carter," his mother promised him, "you can stay with your father as long as you want."

Even though the divorce decree and property settlement was not final, she had the house, property, cash, everything of value to her. She did not need to hold on to him as a bargaining chip. She wanted to get on with her "new life"—attending Austin cultural events with new boyfriends. Carter was extra baggage that slowed her down and complicated her Sunday champagne brunches up at the house with loud questions about why he couldn't go see his dad.

The next twenty-three days Carter lived with me. After school, I would take him and one of his playmates to spend his weekday afternoons with his mother and visit his pets. His mother took his dirty clothes and gave him clean ones. When we left around five, she would head out for Austin or San Antonio. She seemed happy with the setup.

Carter cheered up and the circles under his eyes disappeared. The perfect arrangement, almost too good to be true.

It was.

On May 12, 1983, Carter's mother filed against me in the Hays County courthouse. Her slick Austin divorce lawyer was angry that she had given Carter the right to choose and, instead, claimed I had "kidnapped" my son. The lawyer demanded the court to sentence me to two and one half years in jail. My ex-wife would deny under oath that she ever gave permission for Carter to stay with me. Everybody's lawyers withdrew into a conference room.

Fifteen hundred dollars in fees later, my lawyers got the "charges" dropped and my visitations improved slightly, adding Tuesday and Thursday afternoons. The district judge threatened me with jail but let me off with a warning and approved the modified custody orders. This was going to be one long, tough fight.

"I don't know who she is," Carter said. He was heartbroken

when told he would have to return to his mother. "It's like my mom went away and this other person came back."

A week later I got to see Carter at his Tee Ball game. He was deeply depressed and did not want to go home.

"I've got to get my head in the game. I'm hanging in there but it's tough," he said. The dark circles under his eyes had reappeared. "I'm afraid I am going to get hurt at home. Mom keeps shoving me and pulling me by my arm . . . can't talk about it . . . I'm still here. I'll make it . . . tired . . . my mind . . . I've got to think about the game or I won't have my eyes on the ball."

And he didn't. He seemed to play in a daze.

"I don't want to go home." His eyes pleaded with me after the game. "It is getting crazier all the time up there. They are trying to unplug me from you. But my light is still on."

He kept looking up at me, expecting some answer, some solution. I could not think of a thing to say. "Trying to unplug me from you but my light is still on." What the hell did that mean?

"I feel terrible, Dad . . . I'm tired and my head is tired . . . Mama thinks because I don't say anything that I'm happy but I'm not. I just stay in my room alone while Mom fixes dinner, or something."

I picked up a baseball and we started playing catch.

Carter's final Tee Ball game was May 25, 1983. His enthusiasm and skills had diminished noticeably but he made a great backhand catch on a line drive. He was cheered up by the play.

The last day of school was the beginning of my visitation weekend, I picked him up at school and he proudly showed me his excellent report card and test scores. Carter was happy all weekend, until he realized that he had to go home on Sunday. Immediately, he began to check the time. He stayed on the clock and it tormented him. Time constantly ran out on him.

"She tries to make me think that the divorce is the judge's idea. What does she think, that I'm stupid?" He talked fast, nervously twisting his fingers and rubbing his hands together.

We went to the Wimberley school gym. The principal had given me a key because he knew Carter and I had no place to play.

Often, when Carter had been unhappy at school, the principal had called me and Carter to his office and left us alone to talk and get Carter calmed down so he could concentrate on his classes. This kind of cooperation from the principal and Carter's teachers made school a refuge and helped him maintain the quality of his schoolwork.

At the gym I ran him hard, trying to burn off his nervous energy. He had a good mind and body for sports and a wonderful desire to learn, to be coached. He wanted so much out of life and it was flying by—consumed by the lunacy of the divorce. "Do I got to go home on Sunday night?" Carter asked, beginning to cry. "I hate my mom."

"You can't hate your mom, Carter," I explained. "You can be angry at what she does to you—the act. Because you have to remember what makes you mad or soon you'll just be mad all the time. But you can't hate your mom. It's bad for you. It hurts you to hate your mom."

"Dad? Are you gonna stop fighting for custody of me in the divorce?" Carter asked.

"Do you want me to stop?"

"No!" He looked at me. "It's not much fun talking about something that you're trying to pretend isn't even happening."

"I'm sorry, Carter. But it is happening, and, if we are going to make our lives work, we gotta remember and understand what happens to us, even the unhappy things like divorce. If we forget what has happened we forget who we are."

"It's sort of like being in a trance, isn't it, Dad?" Carter was sad and began to cry again.

I held him and let him cry. He finally asked me to carry him to bed. As I tucked him in, Carter looked up at me. "My puppy, Rosie, died," he said.

11 ◊ The Deal

SIX MONTHS HAD PASSED, and Carter's mother's lawyers kept delaying the divorce and the custody hearing. The longer the modified orders stayed in place, the greater the odds they would become the permanent orders. The odds against me getting custody had long since passed to infinitesimal. My lawyers were telling me that the number of times a court changed custody in Texas could be counted on one hand.

The time Carter and I were spending apart was torture and the extra time we snuck together (the Modified Orders allowed me to see him only two weekends a month and for five hours twice a week) was getting more and more dangerous. Between that and all the specious charges, jail time was a very real possibility.

Carter and I spent one whole weekend discussing the situation with Sonny Gold. The three of us decided that if we could get liberal visitation, and guarantees that his mother would keep him in Wimberley, we would settle. Sonny called my ex-wife and negotiated the whole deal over the phone in less than an hour. It was mid-July 1983.

Carter's mother accepted a settlement that gave Carter and me the rest of the summer—an immediate seven weeks together—custody weekends that lasted from Thursday after school until Monday morning, plus every other Tuesday and Thursday from the end of school to seven P.M. In addition, Carter got 20 percent ownership of the house and I got the promise that my ex-wife would not sell the house and move Carter away from me. I agreed and it was done.

Carter and I spent the seven weeks together. The divorce decree was signed in early August and Carter returned to school in Wimberley in the fall.

One day, Carter's mother called me at my office. She asked me to come to the house to talk. It was my visitation day and I assumed she wanted to adjust some timing in the handoff. As usual, I was wrong.

I drove Carter and his playmate Cary up to the house. His mother was sitting in a chair on the front deck. "I am putting the house on the market and Carter and I are moving to Austin," she announced.

I was stunned. "You promised not to sell the house or move Carter away. It was the most important part of the settlement. You can't—"

"My lawyer says I can do whatever I want," she cut me off.

She was right. She could and would do anything she wanted. Over and over again. This was divorce and she was the custodial parent.

"I'm selling the house and buying a condo in Austin."

Great! A condo in Austin in a real estate market that was softer than Cream of Wheat. When the oil boom collapsed into $200 billion in bad loans it was gonna be panic city in Texas. The bottom was falling out of the market. I wasn't even sure she could sell the house. But I couldn't take the chance.

"If you want to buy me out, you will have to come up with the sixty-five thousand dollars in cash by the end of the week to pay down," she said.

"I can't get that kind of money," I said. "You cleaned out all the bank accounts and safe-deposit boxes. When people call for me about writing jobs you tell them I don't live there and hang up. If one of my checks ends up in your mail, you cash it and keep the money. How the hell am I ever gonna get sixty-five thousand dollars."

"Are you accusing me of stealing?" she asked.

"What would you call it?" I said.

"I don't have to take your shit!" she snapped, bolting out of her deck chair and heading for the front door.

She slammed the door and I was left outside with Carter and Cary. We went into the backyard for about twenty minutes. Then we heard "Carter! Cary!" Coming out of the back door she was bringing them chocolate milk, and after she had handed them their glasses, she returned to the house.

"You promised you wouldn't sell the house. Carter wants to stay in Wimberley," I said, following her to the sliding glass doors that led from the utility room into the kitchen.

"He'll go where I take him!" She slammed the sliding door to the kitchen, leaving me stranded in the utility room.

"Dad?" Carter stepped into the utility room. He was carrying the two empty milk glasses. "We're all through."

I knocked on the kitchen door and pointed to the two glasses Carter was holding. His mother walked over to the door just as I pulled it open and started to step into the kitchen with Carter behind me.

"I don't want you in my house!" she screamed at me.

Startled, Carter backed into the utility room, just as his mother grabbed the sliding door and tried to slam it shut as hard as she could.

"Get out of my house!" Driving hard with her legs, she was slamming the door hard enough to shatter the glass. Carter was right beside me.

I stuck my arms between the glass door and the jamb to cushion the shock. The door bounced off my forearms. My hands went numb. The tips of my fingers brushed her shirt. Rubbing my wrists and forearms, I walked into the kitchen. She continued on into the dining area. Stopping, I leaned up against the kitchen counter and kept about six feet between us.

"You've got to handle your anger," I said. "It will come back on you. You lie to me. You lie to Carter. You lie in court. All you are is your word. Just because you get away with it, doesn't mean that you are really getting away with it."

"You hit me!" she said.

"God will get you for lying," I said. "I barely touched the front of your shirt."

As an agnostic, I didn't really believe God was getting anybody for anything. But she had been evangelical Baptist in her early life. The idea of God reaching down out of the sky and whacking her flat was within her realm of belief. You do what you have to in these kinds of fights. "I mean it. God will get you."

"I haven't done anything wrong." She was pleading her case to the Almighty.

"Calm down," I said. Carter had walked in from the utility room and was listening to her scream at me. "You're gonna scare him. Christ, I thought you broke my arm with the door."

"Well I am scared of you," she said. "You hit me!"

"I didn't hit you, for chrissakes. My fingers brushed you when I shoved my arms in the doorway. You slammed the door so hard I was afraid the glass would break. Carter was standing right there."

Hesitantly, Carter walked into the kitchen, looking from me to his mother.

"It's all right, Carter," I said softly. "Your mom and I have to talk about the house. Go out and play."

"No! No! No! Carter don't go!" she cried. "Daddy's gonna hurt Mommy. Please don't go! Save Mommy!"

"Jesus, what are you doing?" I tried to calm her. "Don't say that to him. Are you crazy?"

I looked at Carter and he looked at me. "Mom's all right, she is just excited. You go out and play with Cary. I'll be out in a few minutes."

"Please, Carter! Don't go! Daddy's going to hurt Mommy if you leave!" she screamed and cried.

Carter looked at her and then at me. I shook my head and he went on outside.

"I can't believe you did that," I said. I stood there trying to figure out what to say. "Do you have the faintest idea how sick that was?" Talking about Carter's best interest with a woman who had just put him into the terrors of the classic Oedipal bind did not offer much hope.

Soon, a real estate saleswoman friend of Carter's mother arrived. She had been called while I was outside with Carter. The convenient arrival of a witness who would gladly commit perjury in return for the listing of a $200,000 house made me realize the danger I was in. It was time to get out.

It was still my visitation day. I walked outside, told Carter and Cary to climb into the car, and drove off. Carter wasn't due back from visitation until seven P.M., two hours later.

As we drove out of the driveway, Carter stood leaning against me on the car seat. "Why was Mom yelling for me to save her?" he asked.

I paused, trying to frame the right answer, but he continued. "What did she expect me to do?" Carter shook his head and smiled. "Go get my plastic sword?"

Carter and Cary laughed at the idea of Carter attacking me with a plastic sword and were soon wrestling in the backseat.

When I returned with Carter the house was empty. Nobody answered the phone for the next two days.

I called my attorneys and told them to prepare for the worst. And it was the worst: assault and battery, and kidnapping. She swore I had grabbed her by the throat, slammed her into the kitchen walls, and tried to kill her.

I hired more lawyers to defend me against the assault and kidnapping charges. Then I reopened the suit for change of custody. The fight was back on. Court dates were set. It was going to be an expensive long shot at best.

12 ◇ Waiting for Judgment Day

CARTER WAS SITTING ON the front steps with his baseball glove and ball when I drove up the long, curving driveway. "Let's go up to Sonny's house and play catch," Carter said as he scrambled into the front seat. "Let's go before she comes out and stops us."

"She can't stop us. It's our weekend together."

"Let's just get going," Carter said, not at all convinced we had any guaranteed rights.

The Golds' yard was not the most perfect baseball ground—mostly rough, rocky, caliche dotted with a few cacti and some clump grass. I threw Carter pop-ups and long fly balls. The mistake was trying to go to grounders.

"Okay, keep your glove down and keep your eyes on the ball," I told him. "Don't turn your head when the ball gets there. You don't want to get hit on the temple or behind the ear."

Carter was crouched, playing the grounder I had slung with good force. He moved over to block the ball, making sure that if he missed it his body would keep it from going any farther. He was down, knees bent, glove at the ready, when the ball hit the mound of clump grass about three feet in front of him, bounced over his mitt, and hit him square on the nose.

Blood flew everywhere and streamed out of his nostrils. He wiped it on his sleeve and picked up the ball. It was an awful sight.

I ran over to see how badly I had damaged him. Blood was smeared all over his face and down his T-shirt. "Carter, I'm sorry. I shouldn't have thrown the ball so hard. Let me see your nose."

He bent his head back, thrusting his nose toward me for inspection. It didn't seem broken nor did the cartilage seem torn or dislocated. The blood continued to drop onto the caliche.

"I didn't turn my head," he said. He handed me the ball. His eyes brimmed with tears. He wasn't crying. It was reflex from the ball smashing the shit out of his nose.

"You sure didn't," I said. "I am really sorry. Let's get that bleeding stopped. Come on, we'll go inside."

"Okay. But can we play after my nose stops bleeding? I did exactly what you told me. I never took my eye off the ball. I didn't turn my head. So can we play later? Can we?" Carter asked.

"Sure." I looked down at the bloodied seven-year-old. "You played the ball exactly right. You did what I told you."

He had followed my instructions perfectly and look at the bloody mess I had made of his face.

"Can we play more? I want to be a good player." Blood still

streaming from his nose, Carter walked beside me toward Judge Gold's house. "You just show me what to do and I'll do it. Can we play? Puuleeeeze?"

I looked into the big sad eyes, the bloodied, tear-streaked face, and skinned nose. With perfect clarity, I realized how difficult raising Carter was going to be. No matter what happened, there wasn't going to be anyone to absolve me and forgive me for all the mistakes I would make. It would be difficult in any circumstances. But while fighting an ongoing battle for custody, it was going to be a nightmare of screwups, court battles, and jail sentences.

Already, people were telling me I was stupid and selfish to fight for custody. I was hurting Carter and should stop before I did irreparable damage. I was on my own trying to keep Carter treading water while everybody kept handing us anchors, then talked about how "resilient" kids were. And although only a few friends stayed the course in Texas, all my friends and family in Michigan put themselves on the line, personally and financially, to keep Carter and me from sinking.

Was I strong enough to get through a lifetime of three-in-the-morning regrets and fears, high temperatures, store throats, colds, and night terrors?

Forgiving myself was not a skill that I had tried to cultivate while playing college basketball or professional football. In the fast lane of world-class sports, New York publishing, and Hollywood movies, being forgiving of oneself or others was a dead-bang route to total failure.

◇

Eventually, I was called to court to answer for my "alleged" crimes. The judge found me guilty and sentenced me to a year in jail. He made me serve two days, then suspended the rest with the proviso that I would be immediately jailed for the full term should my ex-wife notify the court of any misbehavior on my part.

The real estate lady had perjured herself by saying she had seen bruises on my ex-wife's neck where I supposedly throttled her. The joke was on the real estate lady. After lying in court for Carter's mother, she still didn't have the house listing. In fact, the Texas real estate market was so bad, the house didn't sell for ten years.

13 ◇ The Fast Lane

THE YEARS I PLAYED Big Ten basketball at Michigan State I was able to keep my life pretty much under control. The decisions weren't difficult. They certainly weren't subtle. I could either work like a dog on the basketball floor and use my little free time to study until I went blind. Or, I could have a social life, join a fraternity, drink, run, and probably get kicked off the team and/or flunk out of school.

The first choice was no bed of roses. But, I took it. My college memories revolve around the basketball floor out in the middle of Jenison Field House, my apartment, my roommates, my teammates, my coaches, a couple of professors, classrooms, and the constant feeling of always being tired, hungry, and anxious.

Except for my roommates and the basketball games, it wasn't a lot of fun. Long before "get a life" became a popular rejoinder, I was among the first people without a life. It was not surprising that other athletes took a different course. They seemed to have a lot more fun and not all of them got kicked off their teams or flunked out of school—but many of them did and few graduated.

Eventually a lot of us went on to the NFL or AFL and in 1964 Michigan State had more players in pro football than any other Big Ten school.

One of two college basketball players, I ended up on the roster of the 1964 Dallas Cowboys; Cornell Green from Utah State was the other.

By 1965, my second year in the NFL, I decided to get a life, put it into overdrive, and keep up with my friends and teammates on the Cowboys. There was a good possibility I overdid it.

First, I dropped out of law school at SMU and began to drink a lot. Alcohol was the drug and fuel of choice in the NFL in those days, although we had access to a variety of others and sampled them liberally.

By mid–1965 I was starting at the flanker position.

In 1966, Dallas hosted the NFL World Championship Game against the Green Bay Packers in the Cotton Bowl and I was rapidly approaching Mach 1.

The Cowboys were suddenly winners. We were all receiving our invitations to become America's Guests. It was a grand and glorious time, made all the more exciting by the risks we all took and the speed at which we were traveling.

The fast lane ended my first marriage in less than six months in 1966. When I had met my first wife at Michigan State, I was still moving carefully and considerately through my life. By the time we married, I had thrown caution to the wind and leapt into the NFL with all the attendant personality changes.

My first wife was a victim of timing and the sudden changes in my life. The problem with the fast lane is that everybody crashes and burns eventually. My first wife never asked for alimony and took only what she brought with her, going out alone into the Dallas business world to make a success of herself on her own terms.

After the divorce I decided to take a run in the really fast lane and began racing production sports cars. I bought a 1966 Shelby Mustang GT 350 Fastback that had been set up for racing by Carroll Shelby himself. She was a daisy.

Since I was able to buy it, I was sure I could race it, just put the pedal to the floor and go. I raced it in Texas for about six months.

Then one day I went to Riverside International Raceway in California. For a short while I was zipping around the track like Mario Andretti–Butkas until the Butkas's alter ego took over on the short straightaway and I missed my line, got all out of shape, and sailed into the pit curve forty miles an hour faster than sanity and physics demanded.

The Shelby hit the rail, at about ninety miles an hour, tearing the front wheel off, and flipping end over end three times. In the blink of an eye, I had turned a beautifully crafted, one-of-a-kind, classic automobile into $400 of scrap metal.

I regained consciousness hanging upside down. I unclasped my shoulder harnesses and crawled out of the shattered rear window, listening to the sound of the gasoline sloshing in the tank. I thanked dumb luck we hadn't hooked up the dual electric fuel pumps. The pumps would have kept pouring gasoline onto the hot engine after the crash and that Shelby would have exploded and burned like the last reel of an Arnold Schwarzenegger movie.

Bruised and sore, I walked away from the car heading toward my mechanic who was running wild-eyed across the track. I tossed the keys to him and gave him the car. I never looked back. Screw that get-right-back-up-on-the-horse bullshit! That Mustang would have killed me deader than Julius Caesar the next time I screwed up. One thing was certain, I would screw up again. I may have been crazy, I wasn't stupid.

I flew back to Dallas just happy to be alive.

Making sixteen thousand dollars a year from the Cowboys plus a thousand-dollar bonus for starting and an additional five-thousand dollars championship money, I was flush. I had my own radio and television shows. Bobby Hayes and I began a successful advertising printing business that paid me twice what I earned on the football field.

Except for the loss of the Shelby, one divorce, and my football injuries (three knee operations, two A/C shoulder separations, a broken leg and dislocated ankle, fractures of my cervical, thoracic, lumbar vertebrae, two short ribs broken clean off my spine, partial paralysis of my lower back, left hip, and leg caused by the team doctor and trainers dragging me off the field with a broken back, plus a few minor dings like the dislocation of all my fingers at one time or another and eight broken noses, things couldn't be looking better.

"Top of the world, Ma!"

In early February 1968, I was wearing a hip-length cast, a constant reminder of how quickly my 1967 season had ended, when I met the woman who was to become my second wife. After our second date, she moved into my house and never left until that strange night in January 1983.

In 1969, the Cowboys traded me to the New York Giants and I took her with me and put her up at a nearby motel. Wellington Mara and Allie Sherman told me that players weren't supposed to bring wives to camp. I told them not to worry, she wasn't my wife and the woman that Fran Tarkenton had in the room next to hers wasn't his wife either.

I figured playing for the Giants in New York was playing in the fastest lane in the NFL. The problem was the Giants didn't know how to drive. Not the players—there were great players—but the owners and the coaches.

Allie Sherman called me to his office early in camp and said he had traded for me because the Giants were going to put in the multiple-formation offense like the Cowboys and he thought I could help him understand it. "All that Dallas shifting doesn't mean anything, does it?" Allie asked. His face was a total blank. I was shocked by the question—this guy was coaching in the NFL in 1969.

"Yeah, Allie." I smirked. "It means everything. Your backs can get a step closer to the hole. You keep the defense from getting its calls until the last second—"

"Okay, that's enough for now." He cut me off with a wave of his hand and kept his eyes down, looking at something on the back of his hand. "And, don't call me Allie."

We never discussed multiple-formation offense again.

I lasted long enough to watch the Apollo 11 astronauts land

on the moon, hear about Woodstock and the Manson Family murders. Playing the exhibition season, the Giants lost every game while I learned to appreciate the quality of Tom Landry's football knowledge, Tex Schramm's organization, and the Murchison Brothers ownership practices. The Cowboys weren't just a football team, they had become legendary, mythic . . . heroic in the classic sense.

Back in Dallas, our printing business had been busted out by "friends" hired to look after the company while I was in New York and Hayes was in Cowboys training camp. They paid themselves good salaries, spent all the corporate funds, and ran up an additional fifty-thousand-dollar debt in a scheme to sell posters and programs at the Texas International Pop Festival. And since Bobby was still playing ball, it was up to me to pay the debt off.

I had to sell half a million dollars' worth of printing. A good salesman sells himself. I found myself and my clients so much more appealing when we were drunk. I drank and sold, until I wiped out the debt and large portions of my liver.

There was no sense slowing down now; I planned to keep it floored until I hit the wall or won the race. There was never any thought of running out of gas, that comes later in life.

I began work on my first novel, *North Dallas Forty*, which, after my taking some side trips to Durango, Mexico, and Beverly Hills, was accepted in the fall of 1972 for publication in the fall of 1973.

Only a guy crazy enough to think he could be a world-class athlete would be crazy enough to think he could write a best-selling novel—I qualified. The paperback and movie deals were made before publication. I began receiving checks immediately.

Bingo! I was in the front row.

I thought I had won the race. Later, I would learn there was another race being run that nobody had even mentioned to me.

Moving back to Michigan, I hid out with my wife and daughter in a house on the shores of a wooded, inland lake about six miles north of Bangor and began to calm down, catch my breath, and try to cool out. Two book tours were mini-fast lane disasters which required extra recovery time and apologies all around. But by 1975, we felt we had our lives under control enough to think about having another child, and on July 16, 1976, Carter was born in Borgess Hospital in Kalamazoo.

Carter's birth made me finally realize that a kid can't choose his parents and that my decisions affected my daughter and my son.

By 1977, my wife and I decided to move to the hill country of Texas up on the Edwards Plateau between Austin and San Antonio. It was quiet beautiful country with limestone aquifers and artesian wells that spilled out full-blown rivers and creeks from steep stone hillsides and creek beds. We bought our house on the side of Old Baldy, a rocky outcrop and local landmark outside of Wimberley, Texas, and I began work on *The Franchise*, a novel about the building of an NFL franchise, set in Texas.

On a Friday midnight in February 1979, I got a call from Hollywood asking me to "do a polish on the final draft of the *North Dallas Forty* screenplay." The movie, starring Nick Nolte and Mac Davis, was due to start production on a Paramount set the next Monday. They needed me right away. I ignored my agent's advice to steer clear of Hollywood and get my novel finished. My wife and I discussed my going west and agreed the "potential" payoff was worth the risk. I hit the ground at LAX, running just like I had in Dallas fifteen years earlier.

Making a movie takes the same mind-set as playing professional football; you're just in a faster lane playing for bigger stakes. In football they can cripple you or fire you if you screw up. Make a mistake in Hollywood and they kill you.

I was back with my foot to the floor for eight weeks of constant writing and rewriting, fighting with the producer and director, drinking and running with Nolte. The Hollywood rat race had the richest, meanest, best-looking, most powerful, and well-dressed killer rats in America. These were the greatest rats I had ever seen.

I seldom slept and had seventy pounds chewed off my ass by

the five-foot-five producer who made me cry once a day mini-
mum. Sometimes I cried all day and all night long. There
should be an Academy Award for the Screenplay with the Most
Tearstains. Finally, after my obligatory nervous breakdown, I
turned in the last Blue Pages for the script and left town a week
before principal photography ended.

Exhausted and confused, I returned to Texas in April. I was
so tired I had to lean against a gatepost to cuss. It would take
me a year to recover and get back to my novel.

I had won the race but at what price? We were running out
of money. My health was shaky. My novel was late. There were
cracks in the foundation of my marriage that I was just too tired
to notice and fix.

By August 1979, the movie was released and successful. I had
50 percent writing credit and the producer and director shared
the other 50 percent. Now, the fast lane led right to my door
in the little town of Wimberley. I had scores of "new best
friends" who drove from Austin, San Antonio, Dallas, and Houston for their daily feeding on "fame" like schools of piranhas.
They ate me alive.

I wanted out of the fast lane forever. I had finally learned my
lesson. Another wreck and I might not even crawl away like I
had from the twisted and smashed remains of my once-beautiful
Shelby GT 350. Self-immolation was a possibility. So, I took the
first off ramp back to the typewriter.

But we were now into the eighties and my wife didn't want to
sit around for two years while I finished a book. She had tasted
money and fame. She liked the sharks and schools of piranhas.
They were pretty and fun and it wasn't her they were feeding on.
At least, not yet. She liked the traffic in the fast lane. She had put
up with a lot in the past; didn't she deserve some reward?

Unfortunately, I could not make her understand that living in
the fast lane was not a reward; it was punishment. She wanted
the ride even if it led nowhere but to disaster. Which it did, at
least, for some of us.

The die was cast and she set her plans in motion while I remained tied to my typewriter working on my novel.

She already had her bag packed, her lawyer consulted, and was ready to head out on the lam, which she did that night in January 1983 when we argued over "Carter's problem" and "the psychologist."

Ten days later, I was out in the street with two suitcases and the clothes on my back to show for twenty-five years of my life.

She never did see that psychologist. Instead, she chose the insane confrontational therapy of the courtroom. All those things did a lot for "Carter's problem."

14 ◇ Home Base

IN THE FIRST YEARS of the custody battles, Carter and I were frantic, relentless wanderers, back and forth from Texas to Michigan. Never in one place long, we stayed low and moved fast.

By the time I gained de facto, if not legal, custody of Carter in the fall of 1985, his early attachments to his family in Michigan were important. He loved his grandfather and grandmother.

My mother was seventy-four years old and caring for my father as he struggled with throat surgery and a congestive heart. She still took on the task of helping Carter to grow into a young boy. The additional work was tiring and soon etched more lines in her face. So Carter quickly assumed responsibility for his own hygiene and getting his schoolwork done, while his grandmother made him breakfast before school and readied his clean clothes every day.

Meanwhile, having raised three sons, my father spent long evenings talking to Carter about his school friends and playmates. And later, after Carter had gone to bed, he listened to my litany of failures as Carter's father.

"We will do everything we can to help you two"—my dad's voice was rough and raw from the recent surgery—"but, I still have to make sure your mother is taken care of after I am gone."

"Don't worry, Dad," I said weakly. "I'll be here to help."

"You won't be any help for a long time." He shook his head. He was saddened at my failure to see the coming events.

In the past, my father and I had quietly disagreed over what he feared were flaws in my marriage—fatal flaws. It hurt him deeply that I had not listened to his advice and tried to work out the problems. Instead, I was insulted by his probing questions. I would have bet my life that my wife would never give up on our marriage—in fact, I did. Worse, I bet other people's lives, including Carter's, his sister's, and my parents'.

But since the divorce, my father never once said "I told you so." Instead, he constantly reminded me that my ex would *always* be Carter's mother and should be treated with that in mind. I often wished my father would gloat and remind me how wrong I had been. I wanted someone to blame besides myself.

"Nobody is ever prepared for betrayal. If they are, they're grifters themselves." It was the most he would ever say. "You trusted her and lost. Now protect Carter."

I remained silent and ashamed. In my mid-forties, I had returned worse off than when I had left home at eighteen. There was little help I could offer my parents or my son.

"Don't take it so hard," my dad said, lighting up a cigarette. "I always told you, life goes on like this for years and then it gets worse."

His laugh degenerated into a cough. He was right. He had warned me for years.

"Now," he added, "settle down, pull yourself together, and get back to work. I've got faith in you. You've fought your way out of some pretty tough spots in your life."

"I've never been through anything like this," I said.

"Nobody expects this kind of ugliness," he said. "Only people you have cared for can hurt you this bad. Just keep moving ahead. If you raise Carter healthy and wise, you will have really accomplished something. You and your two brothers were the best thing that ever happened to me. Family is everything."

◇

My parents moved from Chicago to Bangor in 1940 when my older brother, Charles, was one; I was born in 1942 and my younger brother, James, was born in 1944.

When I was a kid, my first memories of my father were of waiting for him to return from his job working railway mail. He had five days "on the road" and seven days off.

As he jumped down from the mail car with his small black overnight bag in one hand, he seemed as big as all fathers seem to five-year-olds. A handsome man with heavily freckled fair skin, thinning red hair, and rough hands from a lifetime of hard work, he strode purposefully toward our 1939 Ford Coupe. My mother got out from behind the wheel to greet him, and, after promising her we would not move from the car, we all piled out behind her and fought over who got to carry his bag.

Inside the bag were changes of underwear, shirts, his badge, and a .38 snub-nosed revolver. My dad protected the U.S. Mail.

An ex-Marine who had served during the Banana War that put the Somoza family in power in Nicaragua, my father was a loving and gentle man. He taught my two brothers and me to live by six simple rules: (1) get as much education as you can, (2) don't be too anxious to grow up, (3) once you accept a responsibility, never quit, (4) never tell a lie, (5) don't make a promise you can't keep, and (6) never join the Marine Corps or ride a motorcycle.

My earliest memories of playing baseball with my father and brothers were in our backyard in the late forties. He took each one of us, put a bat in our hand, and moved us to the first base side of home plate. "All good hitters are left-handed," he said, and then pitched to us day after day until we could hit the ball left-handed.

The south end of our backyard was walled off by a hedge of junipers which, when we laid out our ball field, became the fence. Over the hedge was a home run. Then, it seemed a long way off from home plate to the hedge, but looking at it now, I wouldn't put the distance at more than thirty, maybe thirty-five feet.

First base was the small evergreen on the west side of the yard that hugged the foundation of the back porch leading off the kitchen of our white frame house. Second base was the circle of yew trees planted about two thirds of the way across the yard from north to south. Third base was the chinaberry tree. To reach third you had to grab the lowest limb and be careful not to crack the branch. Breaking off a branch was an automatic out.

Home plate was a flagstone set in the north end of the yard, right beside a jungle of evergreen trees that closed off the northeast corner of our property and devoured balls at a phenomenal rate. Going in there after a baseball was the equivalent of heading into the Amazon Rain Forest.

Forty-four years later, when you look into that backyard it is inconceivable that you could lose a baseball anywhere. But to us kids, the place was a veritable Bermuda Triangle for baseballs. They disappeared in the yews, the juniper hedge, and under the back porch, where it was dark and none of us wanted to crawl in with the spiders and monsters that we thought lived in that dismal place. Sometimes, the balls just disappeared for no reason at all. They would roll out into the grass, never to be seen again. Or, at least, not until it had rained and the yard had to be mowed.

Often a baseball wouldn't be found until the following spring, when it would just magically appear in exactly the same spot it was last seen. The ball would be in awful condition after spending the winter exposed to the elements in Michigan. But because we had no money and it was still sort of round we would use it. Stiff, swollen, and lumpy, rough with the laces frayed, the ball didn't take long to come apart.

We played with brown, half-stitched balls. We played with balls green from mold and mildew. Hitting them until they just fell to pieces, we would rewind them, black-tape the cover back on, beat the baseballs to mush, then tape them again and beat them some more.

In 1985, when we moved back to Michigan, I took Carter to play catch in that same yard. I couldn't believe how small it had gotten. It was so small that we moved to the side yard to play. The side yard was too narrow to lay out a diamond. But it was long and had good grass—a good place for playing catch. While tossing pop-ups and grounders to Carter, sometimes I would lob the ball up into the branches of the maple tree that overarched the yard from across the sidewalk. He would have to concentrate hard on the ball, as every branch changed its trajectory, angle, and speed.

I guess he learned well enough. I never gave him another bloody nose.

◇

One morning in the spring of 1988, my father's congestive heart began to fail him. He was having difficulty breathing and we considered taking him to the hospital.

Not yet twelve years old, Carter was in sixth grade. "I'm not going to school," Carter said. "I don't want to go off, then come back and find Grandpa has gone away. I am staying here."

I told him his grandfather would be all right and guaranteed that he would be waiting for him. Carter climbed in the car and I took him to school. We made plans for me to pick him up with the Finch twins after school.

A little before three o'clock, I left my father sitting in the living room and started out to pick up Carter. First, I made a stop at the grocery store. When I walked in, there was a message to get right back home.

My father had died of heart failure within minutes after I left the house.

Carter and the Finch twins arrived only moments after the

ambulance had taken Carter's grandfather away. Despite all my assurances to the contrary, Carter returned from school only to find his grandfather dead and gone.

Carter and Ben and Eric stood in the front yard with me while I explained what had happened. They looked blankly at me and then said they were going for a walk. Fifteen minutes later Lori, the twins' mother, called me. "What has happened to the boys?" she asked me. "I just got a call. Somebody saw Carter, Ben, and Eric all down at the corner of Cass and Monroe crying."

The three boys shared their grief together without adults. They had that kind of friendship.

When Carter returned, the crying was over and he set about helping his grandmother grieve the death of her husband of nearly sixty years.

◇

Two years later, my older brother, Charles, was diagnosed with advanced throat cancer. He moved home while he underwent treatment. The prognosis was not good and the progression of the disease was rapid and ugly. Charles just seemed to wither away from minute to minute.

"Uncle Charlie is going to die isn't he, Dad?" Carter asked one day in the fall of 1990. He was watching my brother walk out of the room. His clothes just hung on him.

"Yes, he is," I said. "But I don't think he is afraid."

"How do you know?"

"Because he told me the other day when I took him to the hospital for treatment," I explained. "Your uncle understood and accepted the fact he was going to die. He was dealing with it like a man. We all hope we can be that brave when we die."

"I don't want him to die."

"Me either," I said. "But we don't always get what we want."

"Yeah, I know." Carter frowned. Of course, he *knew*. Carter hadn't been getting what he wanted since January 1983.

Two nights later, I went to check on my brother at two A.M.

and found that Charles had died sometime between then and midnight, when I had last checked on him. After sitting with him for a couple of minutes—saying good-bye, thinking of things we had done together and of those things we had planned but never got around to doing—I composed myself and began to formulate the plans for dealing with those things that necessarily come with that awful finality of death.

I needed help. So first I woke up Carter. "Carter," I said, after he had come fully awake and studied my face. "Carter—"

"My uncle Charlie died," Carter interrupted, his face wrinkled from sleep, his mind alert. "I knew it. I could tell last night. Something was gone from him."

"Yeah." I sighed and exhaled, puffing up my cheeks.

"Oh, Grandma is gonna be real upset," Carter said, looking at me. "Boy, she is gonna be sad. What should we do?"

"Well," I said, "I'm going to call the funeral home. Then, I will call Jan and Ed next door to ask them to come over to be with your grandma when I wake her and tell her about Charlie."

"Grandma likes them. That's a good idea," Carter said. "Should I go be with Uncle Charlie?"

The question surprised me. "What do you think?"

"I better go be with him until you wake up Grandma," Carter said. "She wouldn't want him to be all alone."

Carter walked back toward Charlie's bedroom and I began to dial the phone. My mind searched for the words I would need to wake and tell my mother that her firstborn son had died a month short of his fifty-first birthday.

Carter stayed in the dark bedroom and sat next to his uncle until everything was arranged. Then he rejoined me while people came and went and his grandmother grieved.

He was fourteen years old.

15 ◇ Spring 1991—The First Connie Mack Team

IN THE LATE SPRING of 1991, I was watching Carter's freshman baseball game, when varsity players Josh Carpenter and Mike Wisniewski walked up. Josh had grown up in Bangor and was a natural athlete who starred in baseball, basketball, and football. Nuke Wisniewski had moved to Bangor from Chicago that year and was a freshman with Carter. But he had such athletic skill that he could play any sport at the varsity level. When Mike graduated, he would be ranked as a high school pitcher—seventh in the Nation All-time in Strikeouts, averaging two strikeouts an inning for four years.

Josh and Mike were talking to Greg Seymour whose son Brian was also playing on the freshman team with Carter. I was behind the bleachers back of home plate.

Greg then walked over to me. "Pete! These two guys want to play summer baseball," he said, pointing to Mike and Josh. "We don't have a Connie Mack program in our plans. If we get one, will you coach?"

I didn't respond. Carter was one strike deep at bat. My heart was in my mouth. He fouled off the next pitch.

As the pitcher delivered, Carter came out of his crouch, started to swing, and pulled back. Ball one. He held up one hand until he was comfortably back into the batter's box. The pitcher wound up and threw again. Carter stepped out, the bat started forward, and he singled into left. Carter rounded first base, pulled off his batting gloves, and stuck them into his back pocket. He was safe again. Safe one more time. My heart soared.

"Pete, I don't even think we can get into a league," Greg continued. "It's too late. But if we do, they'll need a coach."

I kept watching the game and thought about the upcoming summer. I knew that after the first two weeks Carter would be bored. He was only fourteen and couldn't drive. The social activity in Bangor was nil, unless burglary was considered a failed attempt to meet people.

"What age group is Connie Mack?" I asked.

"Sixteen to eighteen," Greg replied.

"Carter'll only be fifteen in July. I'm not going to coach in a league he can't play in."

"You can play younger kids."

"All right," I agreed, "I'll coach. I'm not going to buy baseballs and bats and take care of the field. Somebody else has to do that."

"No problem," Greg said. "That'll be handled by the community recreation program."

Why did I not believe that would happen?

I looked over at Josh Carpenter and Mike Wisniewski. They were both exceptional talents and they were the ones who wanted to play. Add the Finch twins, Carter, Brian Seymour, outfielder Steve Leonard, Mike Wisser and Andy Murray as additional pitchers, and Chris Christian at catcher. There were only ten players. But they were talented. I had been watching or coaching most of them in summer baseball since fifth grade. We just might have a really good team.

Besides, the greatest of my pleasures as a coach was to sit in the dugout and listen to Carter laugh. His unrestrained glee gladdened me. I would sit alone at the end of the bench, pretending to be studying the score book and let his laughter wash over me like warm water. It was a marvelous experience.

"Yeah, I'll do it," I said, acutely aware of how much I enjoyed being included in by the kids. A coach with the mentality of a batboy, I just liked to hang around with them. Connie Mack baseball would allow me to be one of the guys for one more summer, at least. There was no way I would pass that up, no matter how much work was involved.

Three weeks later, in the late spring of 1991, Greg Seymour

called and said we were in a Connie Mack league south of Bangor in Eaton Park, a suburb of Benton Harbor–St. Joseph. "You'll be up against bigger programs," Greg said. "But with the kids you got, you'll do okay."

A week after school ended, Mike Wisniewski took his phenomenal left arm to Chicago to work for the summer, Brian Seymour decided not to play, and the Finch twins picked blueberries instead of playing baseball. And, halfway through the season, Josh Carpenter quit to take a job in a lumberyard in South Haven.

Still, I had Carter at second, pitchers/infielders Mike Wisser and Andy Murray, catcher Chris Christian, infielders Matt Skarritt and Steve Leonard, and outfielders Shaun Eisner and Eric Buskirk. Before the season started, I grabbed five talented boys from nearby Bloomingdale (a town smaller than Bangor) to fill out the roster. It wasn't a bad team.

Wearing three-dollar hats and five-dollar polyester T-shirts that melted in the summer heat, we staggered south toward Eaton Park, looking like the swamp rats we were, and commenced to win baseball games. The kids loved playing in Eaton Park because it had lights for night games and a public address system announced the starting lineups. This was major league to Carter and the Bangor boys.

Over the summer of 1991 we put together a winning team and won the Eaton Park Championship and qualified for a seed in the AABC Connie Mack State District Tournament to be played at Western Michigan University in Kalamazoo. This was to be our first bewildering confrontation with the mighty Kalamazoo Maroons organization, the baseball terrors of Michigan. It was the beginning of a strange rivalry that would last until the end of the summer of 1993. The high-class kids versus the hillbilly boys.

It had its moments.

16 ◇ The First State Districts

THE JULY 1991 AABC Connie Mack State District Tournament was just grand and glorious, pitting teams from Kalamazoo, Jackson, Paw Paw, Climax-Scotts, Coldwater, and Bangor in a four-day battle for the right to be called the best team in southwest Michigan.

The Kalamazoo Maroons boasted nearly as many sponsors as they did players. The Jackson team was sponsored by Wendy's hamburgers and was called Jackson Wendy's. (There were many Connie Mack teams throughout the country sponsored by Wendy's.) And except for Climax-Scotts and Paw Paw, the other teams looked like serious powerhouses. Like the Maroons.

"The Kalamazoo Maroons are one of the top Connie Mack teams in the country," Carter said. He had been following them for a couple of years. "They got Ryan Topham, Shane Sheldon, and Derek Jeter."

"Who is Derek Jeter?" I asked. "I've heard the name . . ."

"Just about the best high school player in the nation," Carter said. "Jeter's going to the majors for sure next year. He's only a junior at Kalamazoo Central."

The Kalamazoo Maroons AABC Connie Mack program was sponsored and kept flush with cash by individuals, businesses, and corporations from the Kalamazoo–Battle Creek area, including doctors, lawyers, insurance companies, car lots, real estate companies, and a variety of service industries. As well run as a small professional program with good community support, the program had a loyal following of parents and fans. Its Connie Mack teams, the Maroons and Kalamazoo Too, nourished with lots of money, good coaching, and community support, consisted of a total of about forty very talented kids and several great players. There was also the developmental Babe Ruth all-star team of sixteen-year-olds sponsored by RATHCO, a construction company. RATHCO competed in the AABC Babe Ruth Tournaments.

The Maroons were the first-line Connie Mack team. There was no secondary interest. If you played for the Kalamazoo Maroons, you played or practiced baseball every day as long as the Connie Mack season lasted. Some parents signed limited guardianship of their children over to the Maroons for the baseball season. With about four coaches and Mike Hinga as a general manager, the Maroons played fifty to sixty games in a summer, traveling as far as Kentucky to participate in tournaments. Their budget ran in the tens of thousands of dollars.

Our budget ran a little over two hundred dollars, plus gas, oil, and cigarettes. Carter's grandmother paid for most of it.

The number two team, Kalamazoo Too, was pretty good in its own right. KTOO wore the Maroons uniform and played a similar schedule without the southern trip. Made up of kids from Portage Northern and Central, Grand Valley, Comstock, Kalamazoo Central, Kalamazoo Loy Norrix, Mattawan, and one kid from Proctor, New Hampshire, the Kalamazoo Too Players had just missed making the Maroons squad and were excellent athletes. KTOO sometimes beat the Maroons and was capable of beating a lot of the big-city Connie Mack teams in Michigan, Indiana, Ohio, and Illinois.

The Maroons held tryouts for top players from Kalamazoo and the surrounding areas, including other states. In that summer of 1991, besides Derek Jeter, Ryan Topham, Shane Sheldon, and other top high school players from the Kalamazoo–Battle Creek area, they had a kid from the Texas Marine Academy and a player from Georgetown College in Kentucky.

The Maroons certainly had a team in 1991. A total of twenty of the best players around and an exceptional starting lineup. In fact, the Maroons could field two complete teams of exceptional players.

My roster varied from ten to twelve players, depending on game times and the players' work schedules. By tournament time, as usual, players disappeared on family vacations or took jobs harvesting blueberries. It happened every year.

We had just one eighteen-year-old player, two had just turned fifteen, and one was only fourteen. The rest of the team consisted of sixteen- and seventeen-year-olds. I had picked up two pretty talented players from the Eaton Park League, expanding my roster to fourteen, potentially. Most of our kids worked summer jobs. But once they agreed to play, they worked and still made the games. Even if they had to come dirty, sweaty, and wearing their work clothes. I appreciated their dedication.

Carter had talked about getting a job that summer.

"Don't be in a hurry to grow up and get a job," I told him, giving advice my father had given me. "You are only young once. Play ball as long as you can. You'll have to work soon enough. Once you do, it lasts the rest of your life."

◇

I played Big Ten basketball and then NFL football until I was twenty-seven years old, and when it was over, it seemed like it had lasted only a moment. During those years, I watched players at every level of competition, including the pros, fail to comprehend how quickly it all could end.

◇

"These teams are tough." Carter was leafing through the tournament program and the rosters of the competing teams. "The maroons have ten guys over six feet tall. We have one."

"Bangor is tiny compared to Kalamazoo, Jackson, and Coldwater," I said. "They all have big programs drawing all-stars from scores, maybe hundreds, of high school players. Look there—Jackson picks up players from eight different high schools, plus having Dave Thomas and Wendy's supporting them."

"Dad"—Carter frowned—"the Wendy's in Jackson supports the team, not every Wendy's in America."

"I know," I said. "But, how many are there in Jackson and how many Wendy's teams are there playing across the country this weekend?"

"This is a strong tournament and we need every player and break we can get," Carter said, dismissing my Wendy's conspiracy to control the AABC.

"You guys are tough." I rubbed Carter's shoulders. "You'll do okay, don't worry."

"I'm not worried. I can't wait to play," Carter said with a big smile.

Arriving at three o'clock for our scheduled four o'clock game against Grand Rapids, we looked pretty ragged. The Bangor team was dressed in variously colored and styled "gimme" hats, shirts, shorts, sweats, and old baseball pants and jerseys swiped from various high school programs. (The American Amateur Baseball Congress which oversees Connie Mack play and sets tournament rules was pretty finicky about appearances. All teams were to have nice, neat matching uniforms. Outfits running in the hundred-dollar-per-player range were preferable. We had already violated tournament rules simply by showing up. It wouldn't be the last time we broke a rule or two.)

"Look at this place," Carter yelped as we drove into the stadium parking lot. "It looks like a major league park. Dad, are you sure this is where we're gonna play?"

Suddenly, this tournament was even more important, because it was being played at Western Michigan University's baseball stadium, a beautifully manicured, high-class Division I venue. The boys stared in slack-jawed wonder at the field. They couldn't believe they were going to be allowed to walk on it, let alone actually play complete baseball games on it.

"Do you believe this place?"

"This is baaaad, man! I mean, baaad."

"We gotta keep winning so we can keep playing."

I watched Carter, Mike Wisser, Chris Christian, Steve Leonard, Andy Murray, Matt Skarritt, Eric Buskirk, and the rest wander around the field, marveling at the perfect layout of the grass in-field and the deep pastoral green of the outfield. Eventually, they made their way to deep center field and lay down on the grass.

This was a place they had dreamed about—a real baseball field. The fact they were really going to play there had reduced them to a weird sort of giddiness that manifested itself variously in serious talk in low tones, followed by outbursts of unre-strained laughter, ending with long periods of reverent silence as they soaked up the surroundings.

Above it all, I could hear Carter's distinctive laughter. The sound made me happy. He was having another good day in the sun. One more day of laughter. One more day of childhood fun and baseball. Since his mother had declared war on me, it was all I had wanted for him, one more day and then one more day and then one more day . . .

The notable increase in the Bangor players' self-esteem, ele-vated by the fact they belonged in this magnificent stadium as part of this grand and noble drama, made all the headaches, anxiety, and the back pain from sitting on wooden benches during the summer worthwhile. Carter and his teammates had the great, grand, good fortune to have earned their own pew in a real baseball cathedral to play their last games of the summer.

And, before they had grown and gone, they might well return to this splendid church, play their way right into the middle of the magic show. Bangor's nine apostles turning singles into dou-bles, making that white sphere dance in the air, playing their goddamn, christawmighty, Jiminy Cricket magic baseball.

The kids were so happy to be there that I was proud of myself for having been the guy in charge of yelling "Steal!" In baseball as in life, it is often best to take what you can get. Because in a game where a batter who succeeds three out of ten times was considered very good, lots of days you ain't gonna get nothing. Or, even worse, you're gonna get a whole lot of stuff you don't want at all.

Meeting with tournament director Mike Hinga, I learned our

scheduled opponent Grand Rapids had pulled out and was not coming. Instead of awarding us a forfeit, Hinga had quickly called the Connie Mack team from Paw Paw.

I was about to learn a lesson. Tournaments weren't just about games, they were also about pitchers. By then, I had only two left, Andy Murray and Mike Wisser, and I would have to use one of them to beat Paw Paw and advance to the second round against the Maroons the next morning. But the kids so loved playing on such a gorgeous well-groomed field that they were thankful for the privilege of playing an extra game.

It was a great day.

17 ◇ Game One—Paw Paw

WESTERN MICHIGAN UNIVERSITY'S COVERED grandstands, painted a deep green, ran from first base around to third and were built into a natural bowl formed by a wooded ridgeline. Carter and his teammates were taking batting practice in the cages down the left field line.

As I sat in the dugout of this grand theater of baseball with all of its possibilities, all its chances for glory, I felt an added tone and texture to this event. This day had meaning and we were in a state of grace.

When the game started, all my circuits were overloaded. I wanted to feel everything, even if it meant burning up a few brain cells and blowing out a few transformers.

"Isn't this great, Dad?" Carter said. He wasn't expecting a reply. "I never thought I would get to play in such a great stadium. I want to go to college and play baseball here."

"You just turned fifteen. We've got lots of time left to think about college," I said. Just concentrate on beating Paw Paw." We were up to bat. "You'll get to play at least two more games on this field."

"Two more games, that is too great," he replied, suddenly hugging my neck and kissing my cheek. "Thanks, Dad."

"For what?" I was startled. "I didn't do anything but drive you guys over here."

"Thanks for the team and everything."

Chris Christian was batting. Mike Wisser was on deck. Carter batted after Mike, so he started to step up out of the dugout. I grabbed his hand and pulled him back, hugging him against my side. He was such a good kid that it scared me.

Free-floating paranoia ran loose in my brain and suddenly the fear of losing Carter surfaced unexpectedly, with terrifying effect. "He just turned fifteen," I told myself to fight off the horrors that were raking my insides. "We still have plenty of time left."

Mike Wisser singled.

"I'm on deck, Dad. I gotta go." He wiggled to get his thin frame loose from the clutch of my heavy arm. I hugged him tighter for an instant. Then, I kissed him on the top of the head and let him go. He got a hit the first time up.

Mike Wisser pitched a good game and Bangor beat Paw Paw that afternoon. Carter got two hits and made several nice plays at second. Everybody played well and had fun, even Paw Paw.

The forfeit wouldn't have been any fun. Mike Hinga figured Bangor wouldn't beat anybody else and be eliminated in two games. By bringing in Paw Paw, he gave us a chance to play one more game. That's what I chose to believe.

18 ◇ Game Two—The Maroons

THE BANGOR–KALAMAZOO MAROONS game was scheduled for nine A.M. on June 24, 1991. It was a Friday morning, another beautiful day for baseball. When we arrived, the sun was just burning the dew off the infield and outfield grass. There was a slight chill in the air. Stringy, washed-out clouds scudded across the light blue sky.

The sound of leather on leather, the peculiar clunk of the aluminum bats against the balls, the smell of the grass and the gloves, all added to the increasing tension. Everything became more vivid: The colors were brighter, the smells stronger, the sounds clearer.

Every now and then, I would hear Carter's laugh punctuate the air and remembered that it was a good day to be alive.

The Maroons were gathered around their dugout suited out in their finest uniforms. They sure looked good. First-class. Major league. As near as I could tell, the Maroons had two or three different game uniforms, stylish and expensive. A first-class operation, these guys played as good as they looked.

But we weren't chopped liver—even though we looked like it. Andy Murray and Mike Wisser were good pitchers. Andy had good speed and Mike had excellent control, placing the ball where he wanted it when he wanted it there.

Andy would have the difficult task of being the starting pitcher against the Maroons. Wisser played first base, Matt Skarritt was at short, Carter at second, and Rob Houston from Bloomingdale with his rocket arm was at third. These kids made a pretty good infield.

Our outfield was good as well, with Bloomingdale's Harry Ellis in left, Shaun Eisner in center, and Derek Payne, picked up from River Valley in the Eaton Park League, in right. Payne had the kind of speed we would need in that immense outfield. He made several fine running catches that looked like sure extra-base hits.

All these kids had shown they could hit. We had a chance. In the second round and still undefeated, we weren't pushovers.

The longer I sat there and watched Carter, remembering how far he and I had come just to be there with me not wearing handcuffs, the more the possibility of beating the Maroons entered my head.

"The Maroons look good, don't they, Dad?" Carter said, walking up to the dugout. "I wonder if we can beat them."

"We are here and the game is yet to be played," I said. "Any and all things are still possible."

That was the wonderful thing about sports, about baseball. A player was never more alive, never more alert, never more aware of his existence than when the game was yet to be played. These kids played, therefore they existed, and they existed with an extreme intensity. They were definitely on the planet, in the here and now.

"Any one of us could make the difference," Carter said. "Never can tell."

"Hey, bub," I said. "You might make the game-winning play or get the game-winning hit."

So what if he had only just turned fifteen and was skinny as a rail? The outcome was still in the future. Our baseball team had all the qualities of dedication, sacrifice, and discipline. Maybe on this particular Saturday those qualities would be enough.

"It's baseball and it ain't over till it's over," Carter said, and walked off toward the batting cages. His eyes were on the Maroons dugout.

I watched him as he crossed the infield and broke into a stiff-legged trot. If he just had some weight on him he would be a bitch of a player. He soaked up coaching like a sponge and his technique improved so rapidly, it was unbelievable.

Maroons coach Joe Wilmarth stopped by our dugout, introduced himself, and brought up the subject of their starting pitcher. A sure major league prospect, Shane Sheldon had been clocked in the nineties. Sheldon was one of probably eight pitchers the Maroons could have used against us. "He has a little control problem," Wilmarth said. "He nearly killed a kid and is undergoing analysis to overcome his fear of hitting another batter . . ."

This coach was telling me some guy was going to throw a

baseball ninety miles an hour at Carter and the other kids. And, on top of that, when he released the ball he had no idea where it was going? "Whoa!" I put up my hands. "Wait a minute."

"What?" Wilmarth looked at me with surprise and mock innocence.

"I've got one eighteen-year-old player. One!" I said. "The rest of them are only fifteen and sixteen. One is only fourteen. I don't want them getting hit by a guy that throws in the nineties."

"Don't worry." Wilmarth smiled. "He won't hit anybody. I promise you. That's his problem. He throws wild away from the batters. Your kids will be safe."

"You've got other pitchers you could use. If one of my kids freezes in the box, he is dead," I argued. "I don't want any of my kids hurt. Why are you doing this?"

"Shane needs the work," Wilmarth said. "He hasn't done well this year."

"That's hardly reassuring," I replied. "I don't want him using my kids for target practice. Ninety miles an hour? Somebody could get killed."

"None of your kids will get hit," Wilmarth promised me again, and left with a slight bounce in his step.

I didn't like it. Why didn't they wait to use him against one of the bigger, older teams like Coldwater or Kalamazoo Too, or the Detroit Tigers?

"Shane Sheldon is pitching against us, Dad." Carter stepped down in the dugout. Apparently Carter knew before I did. "I've been watching him warm up over by the cages. The guy throws major heat." His soft, gentle face showed no fear, just interest.

"Yeah." I shook my head. "I just heard."

"I wonder what it will be like to try and hit him?" Carter was staring across the field to the bullpen where Sheldon was finishing his warmup.

"Well, just be careful and ready to bail out," I cautioned. "The guy doesn't have a lot of control."

"I know," Carter said. "Maybe we should crowd the plate and shake him up, get some walks."

"Don't go crowding the plate." I was scared. "He could kill you with a wild pitch."

"Aww, Dad, come on, I'm too quick for him." Carter laughed and walked over to the bat case.

"All right, guys," I called the team into the dugout. "You are ready to play one of the best Connie Mack teams in the state, if not the Midwest. You are good players too. Do your best, keep your heads, and try not to make mental errors . . ."

"All right!" They yelled in unison, starting to move away from me. "Let's go and . . ."

"Wait! Wait!" I held up my hands. "They are throwing Shane Sheldon against us. Stay alert in the box and be ready to bail out. He throws in the nineties and has control problems."

"Let's go, we'll get to the guy," somebody yelled.

"We'll crowd the plate," somebody else said. "Let the guy hit one of us. We'll play with his head."

"Don't crowd the plate!" I raised my voice. "He'll play with your head by bouncing balls off it."

The Bangor players moved away from me, totally unaffected by my warnings. I was scared. They weren't.

"There's Derek Jeter." Carter's voice filled with awe the first time the Maroons took the field. Carter knew everything about Jeter. So did all the Bangor players. They thought he was marvelous, and he was.

Wilmarth was right about Sheldon being wild. The Maroons pitcher hit the backstop, the stands, the umpire, and my third batter, Matt Skarritt, square in the ass. My kids had to move around in the batter's box like matadors. It wasn't baseball, it was dodgeball. And, Sheldon threw smoke! Ninety miles an hour with only a slight idea where the goddamn ball was going. He tried to throw it over the plate and was lucky if he kept it in the park.

I finally understood; the Maroons figured they could beat us no matter how wild Sheldon got. Unnerved after Sheldon had hit him, the umpire was flinching and blinking, calling balls and strikes with his eyes closed. He couldn't help himself. It was reflex. After Sheldon hit the second kid, I thought the umpire might warn him. But between innings as I talked to him, the umpire suggested that my batters not dig in.

"It is getting dangerous out there," he said.

"So, my batters should follow your example?"

"This is the Maroons's tournament. Always has been," the umpire said. "Your boys won't beat them and are nuts to be out there crowding the plate. He'll dust them off like a recon Marine. It is scary behind the plate. The catcher has started talking to himself."

But the Bangor players dug in anyway and challenged Sheldon to the end while I hid in the dugout. They never quit. Hell, they never even flinched.

I cringed every time Carter went up to bat. He was fifteen years old, facing speed that wasn't seen all that much in the majors with no control whatsoever. Carter dug in, crowded the plate, and fought Sheldon every pitch, trying to get a walk.

The Bangor players had great respect for the Maroons. Yet after the first couple of innings, they knew they had the right to play on the same field with them. It was a proud day. Mike Wisser and Andy Murray both pitched well. Murray's speed was impressive and he had control. Wisser worked the batter and the corners with off-speed pitches, slow curves, and pinpoint control.

The game seesawed.

Jeter played shortstop like he was born to do it, covering the field against our right-handed batters from behind second base, and showing why the New York Yankees were considering him as a number one draft pick out of Kalamazoo Central High School. As a batter, Jeter had struck out only once in his entire high school career. Then, with the game still within reach, Jeter hit a home run over the left-field fence. The ball had to travel in the air for four hundred feet. It was what Carter called a "dong!"

But the Bangor batters kept coming after Sheldon. They didn't back down or bail out. They went at him, despite my warnings.

It was like watching them tease a coiled diamondback, leaping out of the way when he struck at them. My stomach started to hurt. They knew Sheldon was the Maroons's weak link, and if they had to risk their bodies to get to him, so be it. Despite a couple of boys getting hit in the back and the thigh, they did get to him. Bangor scored four runs, mostly on walks, hit batsmen, wild pitches, and passed balls.

Ultimately, with the help of Jeter's home run, the Maroons's tactics worked; no matter how wild Sheldon got, they won. Bangor did not get beat. The Maroons won. There is a difference. The final score was seven to four. It was a diffident and confusing experience for me. Carter and the team loved the madness of risking life and limb. And it took me several hours to calm down.

Shane Sheldon went on to the majors and scared the hell out of grown men for a while.

We lost our first ever game against the Kalamazoo Maroons. It would not be the last time we played them. By 1993, win or lose, we were driving them crazy. An aging hippie and Bangor's hillbilly boys versus the Maroons's swelligant, talented, young men and their excellent management/coaching and community support.

Bangor's Maroons rivalry was about the wonder of baseball—miracles and myths, tall tales and real successes, near misses and direct hits: The story was equal parts respect, anger, and laughter. Eventually, the games would be history in the classic sense—they made good stories, and the best stories made the best history.

19 ◇ Third Place

THE NEXT MORNING, BANGOR came back in the third game to beat Coldwater, a class team from a big town on the Indiana-Michigan border. Andy Murray pitched his heart out to get us a come-from-behind win in extra innings. The game was a great win and clinched Bangor's third place behind the Maroons and Kalamazoo Too.

The first time the Maroons beat Kalamazoo Too was in the early rounds, sending them down to face Bangor after we beat Coldwater. Kalamazoo Too was an excellent team and beat us handily to move on to the championship round where the Maroons beat them again. The Maroons were just too good for anybody in that district that year.

I got the impression that the Maroons versus Kalamazoo Too battling for the championship was an annual ritual. An all-Kalamazoo final helped to get out the parents, sponsors, and the faithful, and showed how far the Kalamazoo star baseball players had progressed since the previous state district championship.

I sure hoped the Bangor boys would mess that up before we were through. We took third place in the districts, winning two of four games. Nobody except Carter and the Bangor team thought we were going to win more than one game. If we'd had a couple more pitchers, Kalamazoo Too might have been in big trouble. But we didn't.

I had learned a valuable lesson about tournament play: It was all about pitchers.

I was proud of Carter and his teammates. They stuck in there and never folded. These kids were athletes. They were winners. We just needed experience and a couple more players.

◇

The next spring, Mike Hinga invited Bangor to join the Kalamazoo Doubleheader League for the summer of 1992. The Doubleheader League consisted of the three Maroons organization teams: the Maroons, KTOO, and RATHCO (their all-star Babe Ruth League development team of sixteen-year-olds), and us. Bangor was the only non-Maroons organization team in the league and we would have to place second behind the Maroons to qualify for next year's state district tournament.

Apparently, Kalamazoo Too always finished second and it was always an all-Kalamazoo district championship game. Bangor had been invited into the Doubleheader League as cannon fodder for the Maroons and Kalamazoo Too. They would practice on us under game conditions and build up their always impressive winning records. They looked at us as, to use baseball vernacular, major cheese.

These teams scheduled around fifty games a summer in two leagues. Since the Bangor kids all held summer jobs, they never had time to practice. We often sweated out the 5:30 game times waiting for our ninth player to arrive exhausted from work.

What could a bunch of raggedy-assed farm kids possibly do against a class operation like the Maroons/Kalamazoo Too?

The answer certainly surprised me, but not as much as it surprised and upset Mike Hinga. Hey, the guy invited us to join his Doubleheader League and it wasn't my fault the Bangor team played well all through the summer of 1992. Nobody could blame Bangor's winning on me—I was the coach manager. I knew nothing.

We would play our first Doubleheader League game against the Maroons in Bangor for the opening game on June 9, 1992. It would be the first time the Maroons would face Bangor's fifteen-year-old Mike Wisniewski, who had kept his phenomenal left arm in town that summer.

The first-class Maroons versus Bangor's hillbilly boys. Derek Jeter versus Mike Wisniewski. It was a sight to see.

20 ⋄ The Texas Diaries—1984

TYLER

On a beach there was a little boy Tyler. He did not have any friends.

His mom and dad were mean to him.

He did not eat breakfast or lunch. He had a hard life.

Tyler is shy. And Scared!!! *His real mom and dad are dead.*

One day he saw a pretty light.

The light pulled him. He saw ma and pa he went back in time.

But he realized he couldn't live in the past.

So he left accidently through the rong door to the past.

—CARTER GENT, *age seven*

BUSTED

"WHERE WERE YOU YESTERDAY, Dad?" Carter kept his distance and eyed me suspiciously.

I said nothing, surprised at his tense, defiant posture.

"You didn't come get me after school like you promised you would." The muscles of his face were tight beneath the baby soft skin and his expression was torqued hard with anger and fear.

"Mom said you had made an agreement with the judge and weren't going to fight for custody of me anymore. Did you make an agreement with the judge?"

"No." I shook my head. "I did not make any agreement."

"Where were you?" He hadn't moved any closer, worried that I had betrayed him in some side deal with his mother and a judge.

I hesitated, forming the answer carefully. It was now nearly a year we had been fighting this battle. We had lost every round in court. Carter was just seven years old.

"Why didn't you come get me after school?" Carter pressed.

"I was arrested," I said finally. "It took me several hours to be arraigned and to post bond. When I got here you were gone."

He studied my face, searching for clues. Truth.

"You didn't make an agreement with the judge?" Carter's tender child's face still held a hard cast beneath the skin. The dark circles under his eyes were now a permanent facial feature.

"Mom came yesterday and said you had made an agreement not to fight for custody anymore. Did you?"

"No, I told you." I frowned. "I got arrested."

"Good!" His eyes brightened, his face softened, then broke into a wide smile. He ran over to me. "Let's go play *baseball!*"

I hadn't broken my promise and that was all that mattered.

The day before, my ex-wife and her "new lawyer" had me arrested on a criminal charge of "enticement of a child." I was taken to the Hays County Courthouse and arraigned. Fortunately, my literary agent had just loaned me several thousand dollars and I had nine hundred in cash on me. Otherwise, they were set to take me straight to jail. Don't believe that story about getting one phone call—it's not about whether you get to call but when. The judge had no intention of letting me call my lawyer. He wanted me in jail for several days and was extremely angry when I pulled the cash out of my blue jeans.

I tossed the roll of hundreds on the judge's desk and the deputy took me to my car and told me to get the hell out of San Marcos. "These people have gone crazy over this divorce," he said. "They're all sure that your ex is gonna cut them in on millions of dollars."

"Christ, I just posted bond with borrowed money."

"You and I know that, they don't. Get outta here."

My ex-wife's new lawyer didn't get paid up front and that was the reason for the criminal charge. He wanted money.

"Her lawyer will drop the phony enticement charge," my attorney told me later. "They said they just filed it to get your attention."

"They filed a false criminal charge to get my attention?" I was angry. "How can her lawyer offer a plea bargain? This is a criminal charge. This is the state of Texas against me. How the hell did she get the prosecutor to go for this?"

"What she wants is money and you to stop the custody fight," my lawyer replied. "Her lawyer says they can get the charge expunged if you'll stop the custody fight and pay up."

"Bullshit. They don't write this stuff down just to lose it later," I said. "Correct me if I am wrong, but isn't filing a false criminal charge expressly to force me to pay money called extortion?"

"Well yeah, it is." My lawyer seemed unsure. "But before we can sue or get anybody charged for extortion, you will have to go to trial on this charge."

"So? We've been to trial before."

"Do you want to publicly fight a charge like 'enticement of a child'? It sounds like you were molesting Carter. Plus, if you're convicted, you got no case."

"I have no choice." I was furious. "Next she'll be saying I molested my daughter, for chrissakes! Carter will never understand if I give up on custody."

"How many times have you been in court and found guilty?"

"Too many and all of them," I said. "I spent two days in jail last summer after she swore I had attacked her the day we argued about selling the house."

"I rest my case."

"That's *my* point," I said. "She *didn't* get to sell the house. I give in now, she'll come back with something else. Go talk to the D.A. Find out what he thinks."

The Hays County prosecutor had been out of town when the charges were filed against me. When he returned and read the charges, they were never mentioned again.

21 ◇ The Test

To know that you do not know is the best.
To pretend to know when you do not know is disease.
                              —LAO-TZU

EARLY ON, I HIRED a child psychiatrist and a child psychologist to prepare for the inevitable gun battle of experts over "the best interests of the minor child." Since I was being accused of so many crimes and misdemeanors, it was important for me to get less "heated" advice as to what I might be doing right or wrong for Carter.

CONFIDENTIAL PSYCHOLOGICAL REPORT

NAME: *Carter Gent*
SEX: *Male*
DATE OF BIRTH: *July 16, 1976*

REFERRAL

Carter was referred for evaluation . . . to aid in determination of his mental and emotional status pre-
liminary to a custody hearing . . .

BEHAVIOR OBSERVATIONS

Carter is a very attractive youngster, of average height and weight for his age. He was accompanied by his father to the examiner's office . . . He was well groomed.
Carter entered the examiner's office with enthusi-

asm, while expressing some concern that his father wait for him just outside in the inner office.

Carter approached each task with enthusiasm, often making casual and relaxed comments about the nature of the activity. Carter maintained very appropriate behavior and worked with diligence and persistence . . . he put forth good effort . . .

During . . . recess from standardized, structured tasks, Carter displayed open and playful affection with his father.

TEST RESULTS

Carter executed all of the pencil and paper tasks with his right hand. The Bender, D-A-P, and Kinetic Family Drawing were all within normal limits with no remarkable errors or deviations from expected content or form.

Carter's achievement level as measured by the WRAT is considerably above average for his age.

TEST INTERPRETATION

Carter's verbal knowledge, comprehension, abstract thinking, and practical reasoning are all areas where he scores in the superior to very-superior range. He has good grasp of basic numerical concepts and can do mental computations in the superior range of functioning. Auditory attention, immediate memory, and sequencing are in the high-average range.

Carter did mention repeatedly his concern about the divorce, stating "the divorce is my biggest problem." Carter said, "The divorce is really serious to me. It's who gets custody. I want my dad to get custody of me and I'd really feel good about it." When the examiner asked him how he felt about the trial, Carter stated, "I'd be scared if my mom gets custody."

SUMMARY AND OBSERVATIONS

Carter Gent is a very bright and highly skilled youngster. He currently exhibits greater proficiency and fluency in language-related tasks. His nonlanguage scores are notably lower which may owe in part to the special sensitivity of such scores to emotional stress. Clearly, Carter was greatly preoccupied with the impending custody case during the evaluation sessions.

Carter expressed positive regard for the welfare of all persons and animals in both questions and projective stimulus cards. He did express marked and distinct affection and bonding with his father, with whom he identifies strongly.

Carter will most certainly benefit from a more structured and secure emotional environment following the custody ruling. He is a young boy of high intellect and emotional sensitivity. It is in his best interest that his natural inclination to think and feel lovingly of all of his immediate family members be encouraged, despite the family's strained situation. It is also patently obvious that Carter's father is aware of this and is doing what he can to prevent any sense of bitterness or alienation toward any family members.

It is this examiner's opinion that this attitude and effort on the part of Carter's father is a very healthy and healing one and is indispensable to the future emotional development of young Carter.

Signed_____Ph.D.

22 ◇ The Pressure

THE END OF JANUARY 1985 marked the beginning of the third year of the struggle for custody. The odds of getting Carter were never very good to begin with and had gotten considerably worse. But, I promised him I would keep trying. I could not quit.

"I'm mad all the time, Dad," he told me. "Mom makes me tired. She always lies."

I worried what this constant anger and confusion toward his mother was doing to Carter. He was nervous and thin. "Carter, so much has happened. It is impossible to know who did what. You must remember that none of this was your fault."

"I got strep throat again." He handed me an envelope from his mother. This made three out of six visitations that he had strep throat when I picked him up.

The note from his mother said his medicines and dosages were in his Star Wars lunch box. Also, she said she was going to be gone for a week and I should take care of Carter until she got back. Fortunately, I did not have a life, so I was more than happy to nurse him back to health. I called Carter's pediatrician. A fine doctor, he had been caring for Carter since we moved to Texas in 1977.

"He is always sick when I pick him up," I said.

"I have been worried about Carter," the doctor said. "This recurrence of strep is dangerous."

"Carter is very unhappy at home. His mother won't listen to his complaints. He seems angry at her all the time. I can't tell whether he is saying things because he thinks I want to hear them or because she is really making his life that miserable."

"I do counseling for children," the doctor said. "I like Carter. I would be glad to meet with him."

"I am not the custodial parent," I warned.

"Bring him in after office hours. We will talk."

The counseling with Carter's pediatrician improved Carter's attitude. He enjoyed talking to someone he liked without having to worry that what he said would hurt his mother's feelings or mine.

"He must try and understand his mother," the doctor told me later. "That is where most of the tension is coming from. He can't believe his mother would purposely make him unhappy. I will try to get her into counseling and get some of this pressure off of Carter."

I sat up all that night with Carter, rubbing the knots out of his back and neck muscles, trying to get his high temperature down with ice packs and wet towels. The next morning I told Carter he was going to spend the week with me. He was fine by noon and stayed with me until the following Monday.

The next Friday, when I picked up Carter at school, he had a heavy cough, headache, and sore throat. I was shocked at how fast he had deteriorated and that his mother had sent him to school in such poor health.

"I would rather go to school than be at home," he said.

I put him in bed and started him on soup and liquids, then called his pediatrician.

"She brought him in a few days ago," the doctor said. "I explained about stress-related illness and tried to talk about counseling. I am not optimistic about her." Carter was badly congested, and the dark circles under his eyes looked like shiners. The pediatrician suggested that I get him a punching bag. "Get him something to hit to take out his anger," he said.

"I've already got him doing that." I frowned. "Every time I pick him up, I let him punch and kick me, trying to get him to release his anger."

"Does he do it?"

"Yeah. There are times when he goes nuts and starts cussing and yelling and kicking the living hell out of me. I get big bruises on my arms and shoulders. It seems to make him feel better."

"It is going to take a lot of work and a long time."

"This has already taken a lot of work and a long time," I said.

"Stress can cause real sickness," the doctor said. "You're taking a big chance. Have you considered dropping the custody fight?"

"I let her have custody once," I said. "In return for her promise not to move. The ink wasn't dry and she had the house for sale and was enrolling Carter in school in Austin."

The end of February 1985, I picked up Carter from school as scheduled, then called his house from Sonny Gold's office. His mother answered the phone.

"Since I am taking Carter for spring vacation," I said, "I want to work out a visitation schedule up until then."

"What?" Her voice was raspy. She was disoriented. "What did you say?"

I repeated my request. There was a long pause.

"Yeah, you keep him"—she sounded groggy—"keep him as long as you think he wants to stay." She hung up.

The back of my neck chilled, my scalp crawled and somebody was surfing in my stomach. Was this déjà vu all over again? Didn't she make me an offer like this nearly two years before and then file charges trying to put me in jail? Recently she had said I wouldn't get Carter for "an extra minute." Now she was saying "Keep him as long as you think he wants to stay." She was lost in the ozone again and this could mean big trouble. I had to find out what was going on.

"You better be careful," Sonny Gold said. "Tomorrow she'll swear she never said it and you'll be back in jail."

"There's something wrong," I said. "I hear it in her voice."

"Oh, Dad." Carter looked from Judge Gold to me. "Mom had to go to the hospital for her stomach. It hurt and they had to take something out of here." Carter pointed to his chest.

Half an hour later Carter's mother called me back and began to explain; two days earlier she had been diagnosed with third-degree invasive glandular carcinoma. "I called Dr. Whitiker and asked him what I should do." She sobbed. "Please help me. I don't want to die."

"I'll help in any way I can," I said. I meant it. "Anything you want or need, just call. I'll do whatever is necessary."

"Gent," Sonny said when I got off the phone, "you'll help her tie the knot at your hanging. She may not even be sick."

I ignored Sonny's warning and called Dr. Jack Whitiker. Jack had been a friend for fifteen years.

"She was having breast augmentation surgery," Whitiker told me over the phone. "The plastic surgeon severed a malignant tumor. The cancer could go anywhere now. You better get ready to have Carter for quite a while."

Sonny Gold was right to be wary of her. That very day she was asking me for help, she filed suit in Hays County to force me into receivership.

As the days passed, Carter was acutely aware something was wrong. He knew about the operation and he heard playground gossip. She had told everybody but him and was angry when she learned I had discussed her cancer with him.

"Is my mom real sick?" he asked.

"She has a small cancer and they found it early," I said. "Don't worry. She'll get well."

"Maybe she won't."

"Our feelings are all tangled up with the divorce and custody," I said. He didn't need the guilt of her disease haunting him. "If she doesn't get well, it is not anybody's fault."

Carter got down out of his chair, crawled up in my lap, and laid his head on my chest.

"If she dies, I'll get to live with you. I want to live with you, but I don't want my mom to die." He started to cry. I held him to my chest. Did I want her to die? What if she did die?

"Don't worry, your mom will get well." It was easy to say.

He tried to smile; tears ran over his ruddy cheeks.

Carter's mother decided to have her surgery and six months of radiation done in Dallas. All of that time Carter and I stayed in an Austin motel and commuted Carter to Wimberley School, ninety miles round trip, every school day.

When school was out in May, she told me to bring Carter back to Wimberley "for a few days. I am not strong enough to keep him very long. But, I want my vacation time with him now."

Fortunately, her surgery and subsequent treatment put the cancer in remission. Unfortunately, her attitude and behavior toward me and Carter returned to her precancer condition, except that she lacked the overall strength for prolonged fights.

Meanwhile, the judge ruled against me on the "receivership" suit. He set a court date for early September when I would be ordered either to sign over my life to a lawyer of my wife's choosing or go to jail indefinitely for contempt. Though I had done all the Hays County jail time I could stand, I was not going to sign the power of attorney the judge ordered. I was not putting what was left of Carter's and my lives in her lawyer's hands.

How did she expect me to keep paying her house payments, alimony, and child support if I was in jail and my business was threatened with constant lawsuits?

In mid-July, Carter and I moved back to Michigan for the seven weeks of his summer vacation. There was no thought of staying in Texas. We were in constant danger in Texas. In August Carter returned reluctantly. I flew back with him and explained the logistical problems caused by the judge trying to force me into receivership. "The judge in San Marcos wants me to sign a power of attorney next month, Carter," I explained. "And, I just will not sign that paper."

"So? Don't sign it." Carter was tired of all the lawyers and maneuvers. He just wanted me to take him and run to Michigan.

"The judge will have me kept in jail until I sign and I'm not signing—ever. So I can't come back to Texas until I get this judgment of receivership overturned on appeal."

As soon as I returned Carter to Texas, he began calling me in Michigan every night, collect. He demanded I return to Texas. "You promised me you would always be around when I needed you!" Carter was half-scared, half-angry. "You promised!"

"I'll be there as soon as my lawyers in Kalamazoo perfect the filing to move my problems out of San Marcos and into the Federal Court for the Western District of Michigan."

"Dad, I'm scared." Carter called on September 6. "Mom left me alone at the house and I went outside and the door closed all by itself. I ran inside and called you. When are you coming down? I ain't having no fun at school."

"I will be there as soon as I can," I promised.

By the end of September he had lost his patience with me. "Get me out of here!" he yelled over the phone. "You promised you would come anytime I needed you! Why aren't you here?! I hate you! I hate everybody! Goddamnit!"

His calls turned into rages of frustration that would often last hours, as he screamed at me to come back to Texas and get him. I told him he was right, I was wrong, and I was sorry. He used me as a verbal punching bag—long distance. He could only call collect.

Then, as suddenly as the whole custody battle had begun in January 1983, it ended.

It was October 15, 1985.

"Dad," Carter again called collect in the early evening. "Mom says I can come up there."

My heart was in my throat.

"She hasn't decided when yet." I heard Carter nagging her. "Come on, Mom, decide now, please. Come on."

Carter never gave up and had worn her out. She was realizing the stress was affecting her ability to heal from the cancer.

"Put your mother on the phone," I said.

"I can't handle Carter." She sounded tired. "He is so un-happy. He wants to be with you."

"Well, you ran me right out of Texas," I said. "I can't come there."

"I would let him come up there. But I am afraid you won't keep paying for my house, the taxes, and alimony. You'll just leave me here alone to die."

"Send Carter. I will keep making your house payments, alimony, and property taxes." I carefully avoided saying I would ever send him back. "I'll keep paying child support while he is here."

She took the deal and I flew down to pick up Carter the next week.

A few days later my lawyers filed a suit for change of custody at the Van Buren County Courthouse in Paw Paw; no one was to be notified nor was a hearing date set. It was just a safety measure. If she filed against me in Texas, the case in Michigan would have to be heard first. She never filed.

After wasting nearly three years and hundreds of thousands of dollars, she finally just gave up. She had lived with me through fifteen years of pro football, publishing, and movies and she had never noticed my one constant: I do not quit. That is the first rule of sport.

She had everything but the 20 percent of the house I had set aside for Carter. It was cheap at ten times the price.

You can always make more money and buy more things.

You can't make more time.

23 ◇ Spring of 1992

"DAD! DAD!" CARTER CAME storming into my office one early spring afternoon in 1992. He had just finished high school baseball practice.

"What? What?"

"Mike Wisniewski is going to stay in Bangor and play Connie Mack this summer." Carter was excited. "We are gonna have one bad team. We'll spank the Maroons."

Carter was thrilled that Mike had decided to keep his left arm in Bangor. So was I. If Mike could find a good pitching coach to improve his technique, he would easily become a sure bet for Division I and maybe the major leagues.

I was not a good pitching coach.

That meant Mike Wisser, Andy Murray, and Wisniewski had to go head to head with both KTOO and the Maroons's deep, hard-hitting, well-coached rosters of twenty all-star players.

"About ten of the twenty maroons are pitchers, Dad," Carter told me.

The depth of the Maroons pitching staff was impressive and they always threw top pitchers against us, from Shane Sheldon in 1991 to Pat Dunham, Dennis Gest, and Brad Block in 1993.

"Nuke will make us a lot better than last year," Carter continued.

Bangor's thin roster contained most of the same raw, talented, hardworking kids that played last year. Add Mike Wisniewski's great talent as a pitcher, all-around player, and a hitter, plus a year of experience improving the other kids, multiply by their pride, work ethic, and love of one another, and the total would come out to quite a bit more than a sum of the parts.

"It'll be a lot tougher schedule than we played last year in Eaton Park," I reminded Carter. Already nervous about my decision to take Bangor into the talent-heavy Kalamazoo Double-header League, I was fishing for reassurance.

"Don't worry, Dad. This season is really gonna be fun." Carter sat next to me and rested his head on my shoulder. "The guys can't wait to play the Maroons and Kalamazoo Too. We'll beat 'em this year."

Carter had responded with the support I needed. Now, all we had to do was deliver a complete baseball season filled with wins and success. This Bangor team had what it took to beat the very good teams like Kalamazoo Too and the Maroons. We could not go toe to toe five days a week. But, once or twice a week, we would make them work for their porridge.

"Well, the first doubleheader is scheduled for Bangor against Derek Jeter, Ryan Topham, and about five or six of last year's Maroons," I said. "Plus whatever new talent Hinga has uncovered since we last played them."

"Jeter's drafted by the Yankees." Carter was puzzled. "The first high school player taken and the sixth taken overall. In the second round, somebody took Topham but he's going to Notre Dame on scholarship. Can they still play for the Maroons?''

"As long as they haven't signed contracts," I said.

The *USA Today* 1992 High School Player of the Year, Derek Jeter was still with the Maroons. Although he was the New York Yankees number one pick, Jeter had not yet signed a contract. Topham didn't sign until June 1995 with the White Sox, after a sensational career at Notre Dame.

"Thanks a lot, Dad," Carter said, jumping up. "For keeping the baseball team together and everything."

"You have just as much to do with that as I do."

"Well." He kissed me. "Thanks anyway. I'm going to call Chris and Mike Wisser to come work on the roster for the summer. Love you, Dad. Don't worry, we'll beat 'em."

Carter was right. In the summer of 1992, Bangor would win more games than they would lose to the Maroons and Kalamazoo Too. The boys would prove themselves again and again. They beat the Maroons once and lost a couple squeakers to them in the final innings on errors and my coaching mistakes.

After beating Kalamazoo Too five of six games, Bangor won the season-end "playoff game" against KTOO behind Mike Wisniewski's pitching and Carter's sixth-inning double.

Bangor would push KTOO out of its perennial AABC Connie Mack State District Tournament spot. It was the first time in a while Kalamazoo Too didn't qualify.

"We want an all–Kalamazoo Championship Round," Hinga had told his KTOO coach. "You can't let Bangor beat you."

But, it wasn't up to the KTOO coach, Mike Hinga, or me. The Bangor players took things into their own hands, from raking and lining the field to playing the game.

Hinga knew baseball and he hated to lose. He particularly hated to lose to us: a bunch of scroungy-looking, small-town kids, wearing mismatched uniforms, coached by a guy with a five-day beard and a ponytail, who smoked cigarettes and yelled "Steal!" to his base runners.

Kalamazoo Too always played the Maroons in the AABC Connie Mack State District Tourney in Kalamazoo. Bangor could not have KTOO's tourney seed. It was carved in stone somewhere.

24 ◊ The Maroons vs. Bangor

June 9, 1992

"THE MAROONS ARE HERE," said Carter, leaning into the dugout. "They look like they're having a meeting."

The Maroons had pulled into the parking lot up by the high school and were standing around. The Yankee scouts fluttered next to Derek Jeter like bees near honeysuckle. His contract signing with the Yankees was rumored to be close, with a bonus in the high six-figure range.

"What time is it?" I asked Steve Leonard as he dropped into the dugout, pulled off his work shoes, and grabbed his cleats.

"Five o'clock." Steve changed into a pair of sweatpants, a red T-shirt, and a Chicago Cubs cap. "I got off work fifteen minutes early. I wanted to be here on time. Eric Finch is right behind me."

Steve and the Finch twins were working that summer running mechanical blueberry pickers from sunup to sundown, except on game days. The game time was set for 5:30 P.M.

"Steve," Carter said, dropping down on the bench next to him. "Are you ready for these guys?"

"I'll have to borrow a glove," Steve said.

"There's an extra one in the bat bag," Carter said.

"Well, boys," I said to Carter and Steve, "we are about to find out whether I made a really smart or really stupid move joining this league with the Maroons and Kalamazoo Too."

"We want to play the Maroons, don't we, Steve?" Carter replied.

"Sure, we can beat 'em." Steve laced his baseball shoes.

"This could be good experience for you guys," I said. "You'll have to step up week after week to play with these guys and still have a chance to qualify for the state tournament."

"We'll do it." Carter smiled and poked his head out of the dugout to check on the Maroons up in the parking lot. "I want to get back to that baseball stadium."

Carter certainly had himself a field of dreams.

"Well," I continued, "playing excellent athletes game after game will be good for you. The quality of your opponents says something about you. Adversity strengthens. Adversaries define."

"Oh right." Carter rolled his eyes at Steve. "Let's go play catch before he starts on his Nam stories." He called every anecdote and recollection of my past career in sports my "Nam stories."

Carter warmed up his arm. This summer could increase his pride, testing his skills against the best teams. Pride in playing the game translated into pride in himself. Hopefully, Carter would have good memories of this summer, baseball memories of the games these kids played together, growing as a team, growing as young men, growing in friendship and spirit.

Quietly I hoped Carter would define his life in greater terms than I had and not end up in professional sports. But while he was still young, I wanted him to ride the high tide of his athletic skills. He loved the game and the game was best when one was young. It never got that good, that pure, again. Carter and his teammates deserved their small-town summers of self-expression in baseball.

It was why I chose to match the Bangor boys against the Kalamazoo Maroons. They would not get better by playing weak teams. Playing in this league would make or break them. I was betting it would make them.

Of course, as always, there was a risk. The Doubleheader League was tough competition. The possibility of getting spanked game after game by the three all-star teams in the Maroons organization was very real. Losing more games than we won against the Maroons and Kalamazoo Too would keep us from qualifying for the State District Tournament.

The umpires had arrived. The Maroons were finishing up their meeting up in the parking lot by the high school.

Twenty minutes to game time and I had only eight players: Carter, Mike Wisniewski, Mike Wisser, Chris Christian, Shaun Eisner, Steve Leonard, Eric Finch, and Matt Skarritt, who were playing catch by the dugout and talking animatedly. Carter, Chris, Matt, Shaun, Steve, and Mike Wisser had played in the 1991 State District tournament game against the Maroons. They were telling the others what a thrill it had been to play in Western's stadium and how great Jeter, Topham, and the Maroons were, while at the same time convincing themselves that Bangor could sweep that day's doubleheader.

"You guys won't believe that stadium," Carter said, tossing a ball to Steve Leonard. "The grass was like a golf course."

"We've got to get back into the tournament," Mike Wisser said. "I want to play there again so bad."

I watched Carter out of the corner of my eye. In the past couple of years, he had begun to grow rapidly. Having been among the smaller boys in his class in grade school and only about five six in junior high, Carter was now five eleven at the end of his sophomore year in high school. But he weighed only around 130. He was rail-thin and suffered bouts of irregular heartbeat after long periods of physical exertion. His cardiologist could find no physical problem and assured me it was due to his rapid growth.

But . . . was this some residual effect of all the stress and the recurring strep he suffered during the battles in Texas? Had there been some physical and emotional damage that would affect him the rest of his life? Had my determination to not quit the fight for custody done him serious damage? I did not know.

What I did know I had learned years ago. Nobody was going to forgive me or thank me, except Carter. We had been at sea alone together for a long, long time, and in the pitch-dark nights of those fearsome squalls and storms it was he and I: Everybody else was cargo or ballast.

"Jeter crushed that ball." Carter's voice brought me back to the dugout. "He tatered it clear across the highway."

"I thought we still had a chance until then," Chris Christian added.

"The way Sheldon was pitching, we had a chance right up to the end," Matt Skarritt said. "I thought he knocked my ass off. That pitch had to be going a hundred miles an hour."

The others laughed at the red-haired, freckled-faced Matt.

"I ain't kidding," he said, and started to unbuckle his pants.

"Marks on your underwear don't count, Matt," Wisser said.

Everybody laughed harder. Matt rebuckled his pants.

Wisniewski stood off slightly and stared at Derek Jeter up in the parking lot. Mike wanted desperately to be a baseball player. His fast ball was in the high eighties, his curve in the high seventies, and he had a high-speed knuckleball that often crossed the plate in three different directions at once. Since he had the necessary raw skills to achieve his dream, all he needed was shaping and coaching. I could teach Mike the head games of high-level competition but I was helpless at instructing the physical skills of pitching.

He needed a high school coach or teacher who could groom him, and who truly cared what happened to him. But not one coach would accept the responsibility of helping Mike deal with his personal demons and integrate him into the society of Bangor High School. In fact, early on most teachers and coaches made his life difficult, interpreting his shy silence and deep fears as a sullen "Chicago attitude." They had confronted and publicly humiliated Mike when he first moved to Bangor. Then, later, after watching him pitch on the varsity baseball team, these same coaches and teachers treated him with praise and deference. Mike was only fourteen years old and he never forgot this. The result was a seething anger and deep-seated mistrust of every teacher and coach he had. He never knew whether they liked him as a person or a pitcher.

"We're gonna beat the Maroons," catcher Chris Christian spoke. "They haven't seen Wisniewski."

Christian's brown eyes sparkled from beneath his blond eyebrows. At five nine and 160 pounds, he had clean-cut, all-American good looks and an open quality about him. He was a good defensive catcher and left-handed leadoff hitter.

"We got to beat these guys," Carter said. "We don't wanna fall two games behind in the league standings the first day."

"They play in another league besides this one. They've already played probably ten or twelve games," Chris said.

"These guys are tough. Jeter's bad enough," Mike Wisser added. "But they got Topham and seven guys back from last year's team. Plus Scott Wetherbee from Loy Norrix and Brad Block from Portage Central. They both can pitch and rope the ball."

Wisser, a brilliant student and a talented three-sport athlete, brushed back the shock of light brown hair from his forehead. His brown eyes were intense. At six two and 175, Mike Wisser pitched smart. Instead of trying to overpower batters, he set them up, worked combinations and the corners. His father had pitched in the minors and worked with Mike all the time.

For us, the Maroons game would be the first time this summer we had nine guys in one place at the same time. We had not had one practice. The infield warm-up before the game would constitute the entirety of our spring training.

Followed by a large contingent of fans from Kalamazoo, the Maroons came down and began warming up in the outfield.

Eric Buskirk and Andy Murray arrived, and shortly after, Rob Houston and three others showed up from Bloomingdale (Rob being the most talented), giving us fourteen players, a huge turnout. Now, I had to put people on the bench. That was the bad news. I hated that part of the job.

Compared to coaching a seven-inning game, decisions about how and when to substitute were difficult in five-inning games. It seemed like the game began and ended almost immediately. In a tight pitching duel, it was possible that you would not bat your whole lineup twice. One or two mistakes in substitution could cost the game. I knew, I made them. There was little opportunity to recover a lead or to build one.

The first eleven players I had were all good, but the drop-off in skill after that was so great even I noticed it. And, by the end of that first day, I was in trouble with the parents of the boys who didn't play.

Andy Murray would pitch the second game. Last summer, he was the number one pitcher in our rotation and his hard throwing had led us to the extra-innings win against Coldwater for third place in the State District Tournament.

The reason for playing two five-inning games in the Doubleheader League was partly the fact some parks did not have lights. It was also because the Maroons and Kalamazoo Too could get more wins without using up their pitchers, saving those extra innings for their tough second league and tournament schedule. The idea that Bangor was going to win any games had not been given much consideration.

"Am I playing?" Carter asked as he stepped down and stood next to me. He was prepared to suffer the disadvantage of being the coach's son and sit himself, so I would not have to make a hard decision and sit someone else. Carter was a good, dependable player and should play. He knew how I hated to make out the lineup and had volunteered to sit.

By sitting Carter, I could make it look like I was not favoring my son. I had done it before. I was not doing it that day. But I did it another time with disastrous results.

"Yeah, you're playing," I said. "You're at second base."

Mike Hinga came over and we talked for a few moments. I had to buy game balls from him. The recreation program had supplied me with factory seconds that went lopsided at the first hit.

"I'm anxious to see this Wisniewski kid," Hinga said, handing me the balls. "I heard he is really something. We'll take infield practice now. Okay?"

I nodded and looked around for Andy Murray. Andy would have to run our infield and outfield practice. I couldn't swing a bat or throw a ball.

The Maroons took the field. They looked smooth, oiled. They had been playing together for some time. Throws from the outfield to home plate came in on a line. The infield turned double plays with ease.

Carter and his teammates watched. They appreciated good play.

At six three and 180, Derek Jeter moved with rapid ease at shortstop, making difficult plays and throws look routine. That day in June 1992, the Yankee scouts happily watched Derek Jeter and talked to Hinga while Coach Joe Wilmarth handled the infield practice.

Looking older than their seventeen and eighteen years, eleven of the Maroons had already graduated from high school. These guys were a lot bigger than us and there were a lot more of them. Time would tell if they were a lot better.

When the Maroons finished, Andy Murray and Steve Leonard took the Bangor team through infield practice. Mike Wisser took first, Carter moved into the hole at second, Matt Skarritt was on the other side of the bag at shortstop, and Rob Houston had third. The outfield was Eric Finch in left, Shaun Eisner in center, and Eric Buskirk in right.

This was the first time these kids had stepped onto the field together since we took third place in last year's State District ten months ago. They were a little rusty. Easy ground balls were mishandled. Throws went awry. There was no timing. They weren't used to each other. They seemed as mismatched as their uniforms.

"Well, that was your spring training," I said as they came to the dugout. "You are good enough to beat the Maroons. You just can't make any mental errors. Play this game in your head and you'll be fine. Have confidence in yourselves, be thinking all the time, and the rest will take care of itself."

It was the longest talk I had ever given them, excluding the times I took them to eat and was trying to get their pizza orders right.

25 ◇ Nuke vs. Jeter

WE TOOK THE FIELD.

Wisniewski started strong and had leadoff hitter Dave Larson, a six-foot-one outfielder, down 1–2, when Larson blooped a flare off the end of his bat that dropped just outside the infield. The next batter, Brian Bowers, fell behind 0–2, then singled. The Maroons had men at first and second.

Ahead on both, Wisniewski had lost the first two batters. But he looked strong and he would get stronger with each inning. This situation was not unusual for Mike and against weaker teams I wouldn't be worried about him.

But against the Maroons in a five-inning game, I was worried.

Now, the six three, 180-pound National High School Player of the Year Derek Jeter stepped into the box with two men on and no outs. Hinga was happy with the way things were going. The Yankee scouts were beaming. The Maroons seemed set to put little Bangor away in the first inning, with no more effort than it took to flick the ash off the cigarette I was so desperately smoking.

But losing the first two batters had made Wisniewski mad. An angry, focused Mike Wisniewski was dangerous on the mound. It was only the focus part that concerned me.

Nuke threw his first pitch to Jeter, a curve for a ball. Then, he blew two fastballs by Jeter for strikes. Jeter took another curve for a ball.

Wisniewski worked fast on the mound and delivered a curve. Jeter was set at the plate and took a ferocious cut, just as the pitch started to hook and drop. Jeter topped a grounder to Matt Skarritt at shortstop. Larson was running at the crack of the bat. Skarritt reached and tagged him, then made the throw to first in time to get Jeter for a double play.

Suddenly Bangor did not look so ragged.

Next came six four, 190-pound Ryan Topham. This was Topham's last summer of Connie Mack and he was headed for Notre Dame on a baseball scholarship. He looked impressive and powerful as he stepped to the plate.

Wisniewski worked from a stretch and threw a hard-breaking curve and Topham hit nothing but air. The next pitch was another curveball for a called strike. But Bowers had gotten a jump on the ball and was heading for third.

It was obvious that Bowers had any throw beat. But, overanxious with first-game jitters, catcher Chris Christian tried to make the throw and put the ball into left field. It was a mental mistake that wouldn't have happened if we had had time to practice. Bowers easily beat the throw from left field and crossed the plate for the Maroons's first run of the day.

Nuke was up two strikes up on Ryan Topham. He went with his fastball low and inside. Topham grounded out and we were out of the inning. But the Maroons had got an unearned run, and one run meant a lot in a five-inning game.

In the bottom of the inning, Bangor faced Eric Johnson, a seventeen-year-old pitcher from last year's team. This kid had to be safer than Shane Sheldon.

Chris Christian struck out. But Mike Wisniewski drove a double to deep center field and everybody in our dugout went psychotic. Cheering and hugging one another, they began to realize they could play with the Maroons. Then Johnson struck out Mike Wisser and Rob Houston back to back, leaving Nuke stuck on second. Despite the failure to score, the Bangor players stayed pumped up in the field. They believed.

Wisniewski retired the next three Maroons hitters.

We were back at bat. But we couldn't make anything happen.

Wisniewski started out the third inning against Wetherbee. He had him even in the count at 2–2 when Mike's curve hung and Wetherbee nailed it and put the ball out of the park. The Maroons emptied their dugout and met him at the plate.

Furious at his mistake, Wisniewski attacked the next batters, working fast on the mound. He retired the next two on ground balls. Two outs. Nobody on and we're trailing, 0–2, halfway through a five-inning game. Yet, his teammates still believed in him and Nuke just got stronger.

Then back came Derek Jeter.

And Wisniewski was wrath itself, waiting on the hill. He was pissed. He was spleen and gall on the mound.

Derek Jeter was cool and collected in the box.

Bringing incredible heat, Nuke wasted his first pitch, an outside fastball, trying to get Jeter to bite. But Jeter had only one strikeout in high school and he did not accomplish that by fishing for bad pitches. He didn't rattle and was ready for the next pitch.

This ball had to be going eighty miles an hour and looked like another outside fastball. But suddenly, it hooked and dove across the plate from the left side to the right for a called strike. The damn thing just seemed to stop, make a ninety-degree turn and drop right through the strike zone.

Jeter was visibly shocked. So was everybody else, including the umpire who paused for a long moment before calling the strike. He couldn't believe what he had just seen—a curve thrown so fast, breaking so quickly and clean was pure argument against Newtonian physics and the laws of thermodynamics. Wisniewski was throwing according to quantum physics and the Red Shift.

It was a clear strike impossible to hit. Even if Jeter had known it was coming, he could not have hit it.

He clearly wasn't expecting this kind of pitching from a kid not yet sixteen. Jeter stepped out of the box and visibly focused himself. I don't know what he was saying to himself but his lips were moving. He twisted the handle of the wooden bat he was using and stared at the barrel for a long moment, then stepped back into the batter's box.

Foot on the rubber, Nuke had been waiting impatiently and began his windup the instant Jeter was back in. Totally self-taught and throwing with nothing but faith in himself and his arm, Mike appeared to walk off the mound toward Jeter as he delivered the next pitch, blowing an eighty-five-mile-an-hour fastball knee-high right down the middle. Jeter was still swinging when the ball hit Chris Christian's glove, sounding like a gunshot.

Still mad, Mike would not slow down. As soon as he got the ball, he waited impatiently for Jeter to step back up, then immediately started his windup. Confident and showing the character that made him such a great player, Jeter was cool. He dug in and concentrated, waiting to pick up the next pitch as soon as it left Mike's hand.

It did him absolutely no good.

This time Mike turned him inside out with his knuckleball. The ball zoomed toward the plate, moving in all directions at once. Jeter nearly fell in his desperate attempt to hit a seventy-mile-an-hour pitch that was dancing like a deranged hummingbird. He was late and over the pitch. As it crossed the plate, the ball dropped like a rock and Chris dug it out of the dirt.

Everybody was stunned by the third-strike pitch: the umpire, Hinga, the Maroons, the Yankee scouts, Jeter, and me, most of all. It was an incredible thing to see.

This strikeout was only Derek Jeter's second in his high school career. He was devastated. In front of God and the Yankee scouts, a fifteen-year-old kid had just blown out the Yankees's number one pick. Derek Jeter, who later became the 1994 Minor League Player of the Year on his way to a starting shortstop's job in Yankee Stadium, had been completely frustrated by a self-taught left-hander from this little poverty-stricken swamp town in southwest Michigan.

Years from that day, when Jeter was an established star in the majors, every Bangor kid would recount how he was there on that marvelous day. I knew I would. And, as the years passed, I would take more and more credit as the coaching genius who played a key role in this local legend. In fact, I am doing it already.

Jeter walked dejected from the plate.

We were still down, 0–2, in the bottom of the third. The top of our order was up. The first two batters went down. Finally,

Mike Wisser hit a hard single up the middle and then stole second. He got to third on a passed ball. Then Rob Houston drove him home with a single to left.

Bangor trailed by a single run.

Mike Hinga was not happy. He stalked around his dugout. A big man, his temper made him formidable, even fearsome. Generally he talked in a soft, quiet, polite tone. But once you saw his temper, you never forgot it.

Shaun Eisner grounded out to third and we were retired.

The Maroons led, 2–1, in the top of the fourth. Bangor turned ragged again in the fourth and despite the fact Wisniewski's pitching was getting stronger and stronger, we gave up an unearned run on a throwing error.

In the bottom of the fourth, after Steve Leonard drove in Buskirk, Carter drove in Leonard with the tying run. Bangor was coming back. We were tied, 3–3, in the top of the fifth.

Again in the fifth, Wisniewski took down Jeter at the plate.

Derek Jeter had gone 0–3 against Mike Wisniewski. So had Ryan Topham.

First game of the season and Bangor was taking the Maroons down to the wire. Even with no practice and all the errors, the boys showed they could play with one of the top Connie Mack teams in the state.

But good coaching, lots of practice, and more games already played gave the Maroons the edge they needed. They won, 5–3, on two more throwing errors.

It boiled down to coaching. Hinga and his staff could teach, they had actual signals for baserunning, hitting, and pickoff plays. I smoked cigarettes and yelled "Way to go" or, occasionally, "Steal!" Otherwise my contribution was benign at best.

But what Carter, Nuke, Christian, Wisser, and the others lacked from need of coaching they made up for in effort, heart, and talent. They had no fear and they came to play. They outhit the Maroons, 9–5, and all three of their runs were earned, while Kalamazoo earned only two. However, the

Maroons made only two errors. Bangor had six. That made all the difference.

Let down hard by losing the first game, the kids could not redouble their efforts in the second. The Maroons's depth showed. First they battered Andy Murray from the mound. Then they continued to hit against Mike Wisser.

Afterward, while Carter and his friends cleaned up the dugout and packed away the equipment, I talked to Mike Hinga.

"That Wisniewski kid just needs some work on technique. He is an excellent baseball player," Mike said.

"He needs someone to teach him," I said.

"If he gets on a weight program, he will be phenomenal," Hinga added. "He's already good enough to play for us."

"Yeah," Joe Wilmarth spoke up. "We'll pick him up as one of our players from the Doubleheader League for the districts."

"Are you already counting us out of the districts?" I asked. I still hadn't fully forgiven Joe for throwing Shane Sheldon at my kids the year before.

"Oh . . . well . . . yeah . . . sure," Wilmarth stammered, exchanging glances with Hinga. "You guys could finish ahead of KTOO."

It was pretty clear they didn't think the Bangor kids would be able to play competitively in the Doubleheader League with the Maroons and Kalamazoo Too. They felt KTOO was safely assured its perennial spot in the Connie Mack District Tournament.

As I picked up my score book from the dugout, I felt proud of the boys. They had done well against serious talent and, although disappointed at their loss, realized that they had played the Kalamazoo Maroons hard to the end. Smiling at the thoughts of how well the team had played, I walked past the corner of the dugout and opened the gate that led out of the playing field.

A short, stout lady was standing there with her arms folded. I knew her. Her son was on the Bangor team. She was probably really proud of how well the team had done against the Maroons, considering.

"I want to know why my son hardly played at all!" she came right at me. "Those kids all paid their eight dollars. You are supposed to play them all."

"Hey, whoa . . ." I backed away from the woman. "I don't have to play any—"

"I noticed your son played both games," she snapped.

"He happens to be good enough to play both games," I continued, retreating.

"Well, I am going to the recreation board and put a stop to this," she said.

"Lady, Connie Mack ain't a teaching league in Bangor. You want your kid to play more? Then you throw batting practice for him every night." I was now backpedaling like a decent cornerback. "And, as far as the recreation board is concerned"—I continued to back away—"if you can *find* anybody who will listen and do anything, it will be a first in my experience."

Parents. I had been dealing with them for years and few ever acted like adults. Many ruined the sports experience for their kid and some ruined it for all the kids. I knew; I was a parent.

Keeping a kid on the bench was not fun. Believe me.

When the team was on the field, I was all alone in the dugout with the kids I was not playing. Conversation dried up quick and there were baseball bats laying everywhere.

That year Bangor did beat KTOO five out of six games. We even beat the Maroons at their home field. Then, we had to beat Kalamazoo Too again in the seventh "playoff game" behind Wisniewski's pitching and Carter's sixth-inning double. By knocking out Kalamazoo Too and taking their perennial seed in the State District Tournament, the Bangor boys got to play again at Western Michigan University's baseball stadium.

After Wisniewski put on the spectacular pitching show against Derek Jeter, his name went into some computer somewhere and major league scouts started calling and showing up at games.

PART◇TWO

SLIP SLIDING AWAY

Even though you are competent, appear to be incompetent.
Though effective, appear to be ineffective.

—SUN-TZU

26 ◊ 1993—The Coward's Hour

In a real dark night of the soul it is always three o'clock in the morning.
—F. SCOTT FITZGERALD

EIGHT MONTHS BEFORE OUR last summer of Connie Mack baseball, an old piece of ruptured disk began pressing against the nerves in the lumbar region of my spinal cord and pain throbbed out of my back into my left leg. It was residual damage from a thirty-year-old football injury.

At first, it was just an additional pain I had to deal with, an extreme discomfort that caused me problems when I sat, stood, or walked. But, it was bearable, as most pain is, or must become. I had been dealing with pain thresholds since I was eighteen years old. Pain or injury, the eternal question of sport—it was pain if the player felt it and injury if it caused problems for the team.

After a few days, the pain worsened. It began radiating across my whole lower back into both hips and legs. It put the hamstring and gluteous maximus muscles into deep agonizing spasms that knotted up my legs and back from my heels to my shoulder blades.

Soon I could not sit up comfortably. Standing or walking were impossibilities, as the paroxysms in my leg and back muscles would literally drive me to the ground.

Week after week, as I lay helpless on my side, my knees drawn up to relieve the muscle cramps, I began to fear the endless pain that brought dark, nearly suicidal thoughts.

After months confined to bed, I realized that I had reached that point in life where the end was a lot closer than the beginning. I felt that the end had quite possibly arrived. Death had a face and it was mine. It was a terrifying thought.

Since childhood I had always chased off fears of dying by doing the numbers game. Years stretched out in front of me before death became a real statistical possibility. During that long, dark winter, as I lay without purpose or future in the same bed that had carried away my father and brother, the numbers had suddenly turned.

How many years did I have left? Ten? Five? Both were too long to stand this pain. Less than five? It was a very real possibility that I wasn't even going to see the millennium. Just my luck, something happens once in a thousand years and I die the day before. I might never get out of that bed again.

And what would become of Carter? I wasn't the greatest father in the world but I had always been there for him.

Pain and fatigue may make cowards of us all. But I wasn't ready for this. These were very real sums. Many of the men who played in the NFL when I had were already dead. Several were on their second and third heart attacks or were fighting cancer. Right there and then in that bed, I began to fear that I was as old as I was ever going to get.

Life was what had happened while I made plans to take better care of myself. The numbers did not lie: I was already old and slipping fast. Fifty-one and out—cold. I continued to decline. I was not getting better. Thousands of dollars for neurological tests, MRIs, abortive therapy, and unhappy consultations with the best neurosurgeons around had offered less and less hope for recovery.

I had spent the last ten years promising Carter that his father would be next year's champion . . . just wait until next season . . . wait until next Christmas . . . wait until your next birthday . . .

It was next year and I couldn't even walk. Yet, somehow, someway, Carter and I could still have this last summer of baseball. I wanted this one last summer. I had to get back on my feet.

My only chance would be hard and desperate work on the part of my internist and friend Dr. Michael Graf. After weeks of intense diagnoses, prognoses, acupuncture, and analysis of neural behavior, he began to give me reason to hope. A longtime practitioner of holistic medicine, Michael Graf had spent years with me just trying to repair the mindless damage I had helped inflict on my body. He had developed therapy and acupuncture to relieve pain and repair my mind, giving my whole being time to rest and recover from all those years in the fast lane.

"Remember, this isn't just about you," Graf would say when I had worn his patience thin by mistreating myself. "You have a son. Who is going to take care of Carter?"

He was right. Who was going to take care of Carter? I had demanded the privilege without giving thought to the necessity of staying alive to accomplish the task.

Studying all my recent tests, MRIs, and the diagnoses of other doctors and specialists, Dr. Graf examined me and reviewed the medical history he had kept on me for years. He began tracking the decline of my back to its current condition. He spent hours testing and tracing nerve pathways, the chronic pains of traumatic osteoporosis, traumatic osteoarthritis, broken bones, and smashed nerves and muscles.

Using acupuncture, he blocked and stimulated nerves and muscles until he finally diagnosed my current disability as a combination of the damage done to my spinal column playing football and a virus that attacked the nerve paths leading from the spinal cord. After three months of treatments and intensive acupuncture, he got me back on my feet by late April 1993.

I would survive for one last summer of baseball, at least.

27 ◇ Next Year

IT WAS IN LATE May 1993 that Mike Hinga invited Bangor back to play in the Kalamazoo Connie Mack league. After eight years, this would be the final summer of baseball for Carter and me.

"This is going to be the last chance we're gonna have to make it to the district championship game against the Maroons," I told Carter as we again read over the rules and regulations along with the division matchups.

On June 17, 1993, we would open play in the Kalamazoo Connie Mack League against the Kalamazoo Maroons at their home field in Vicksburg. All games would still be five-inning doubleheaders.

"The Maroons have eight or ten pitchers again," Carter said. He was relaxing on the trundle bed. "Starting with Dunham, Gest, and Block and not getting much worse. Dunham and Gest bring gas."

In the next year's major league draft, Pat Dunham and Dennis Gest would be picked out of high school, along with their Maroons teammate Brad Block. All would choose college instead. Dunham would play Division 1 for East Carolina State University.

"We are back down to only Wisniewski and Wisser," I said.

"We gotta find out whether win-loss records or this point system decides who gets into the tournaments," Carter said.

"My guess is that it will depend on how we do against Kalamazoo Too. Qualifying for the State Districts will be trickier than last year." I couldn't shake my angst. Just because I was paranoid did not mean Hinga wasn't out to get me. "They are ready for us this year and going to make it very tough for us to take KTOO's spot in the tournament again this year."

"We had to beat them six out of seven last year," Carter said. "How much tougher can it get?"

◇

The rules determining the 1993 Doubleheader League division winners and league standings were confusing, open to various interpretations and always subject to change. Who qualified for the tournaments depended on these rules.

We were in the West Division with the Maroons, Kalamazoo Too, and Paw Paw. In the East Division were Coldwater, Colon, and Gull Lake (Galesburg had dropped out).

I never took my eyes from the boys' goal of reaching the District championship finals, where I knew we would most certainly find the Maroons. The team had to win the games. And I became the Coach as Proteus. The chameleon. The schemer. Vince Machiavelli.

Trading the logic of the informed for the acuity of the paranoid, I was ever vigilant for ruse, pretext, and sudden shifts in interpretations. Where others saw coincidence, I saw deceptions and artifice, while creating confusion and bewilderment myself.

This was the last summer and I had to be ready for anything. A paranoid was simply the man in possession of all the facts— coaching tips from the man who wrote *Naked Lunch*.

28 ◇ Good Kids

"JOSH CARPENTER IS GONNA play American Legion ball for South Haven," said Carter, sitting on the floor surrounded by athletic supply catalogues. I was on the couch with pen and paper. We were in the living room of Carter's grandmother's house, trying to work up a roster that would make us competitive in the 1993 Kalamazoo Doubleheader Connie Mack League.

"The South Haven coach, Jim McCloughan, is trying to get other guys off our team," Carter continued. "I know he has asked Wisser, Chris, and Nuke."

"Jim McCloughan is the South Haven coach?" his grand-mother asked.

"Yep," Carter said. "He's trying to steal all our players."

"I remember when the McCloughan boys went to school in Bangor," his grandmother said. She had been a secretary in the high school principal's office from about 1958 to 1974. "Their dad was at all the games."

"I remember Mr. McCloughan," I said. "I've seen Jim around South Haven. He is very short with all the attending complexes."

Hearing the sound of footsteps on the front porch, Alex, Carter's Shetland sheepdog, started barking and running back and forth from between Carter's legs to the inner foyer door.

As soon as Mike Wisser and Chris Christian stepped into the living room through the doorway, Alex started jumping up on both of them. I had heard them coming about a block away—Chris had a boom box in the trunk of his car.

"You hear about Josh?" Mike Wisser asked me.

"Playing for South Haven," Chris Christian said.

"McCloughan says he's got Nuke," Wisser added.

"Josh told me he had to play for South Haven about a month ago," I said. "He said he was being recruited by Clark Jones to play baseball for Elmhurst College."

"Where is Elmhurst College?" Carter asked.

"Outside Chicago," Wisser said.

"Who's Clark Jones?" Chris asked.

"He's the guy who was supposed to be running our summer baseball program last year," I said. "Instead, he spent all his time interviewing for coaching jobs."

"Looks like he got one," Carter said.

"That guy?" Wisser was angry. "He was the reason the whole summer recreation program was so screwed up."

"Bangor ranks undependability high when they hire for their athletic programs," I said. "Even summer baseball. Look at me."

"At least, you always show up," Wisser replied. "Although sometimes we wished you hadn't."

Mike laughed and everybody, including my mother, joined in. I didn't particularly enjoy the experience.

"What does any of that have to do with Josh playing in South Haven?" Carter asked.

"Clark Jones went to high school in South Haven," I said.

"Josh said that Clark told him he needed to play with some South Haven kids who were also going to Elmhurst," Wisser added.

"That's not what I heard," Chris said. "Josh said South Haven's coach was more serious about baseball than you were."

"Well . . . sure . . . There is always that," I said. Although being compared negatively to the South Haven coach McCloughan was a new experience, I was not surprised by the opinion that I wasn't serious enough. "Josh was also pretty sure Clark Jones promised him an eighteen-thousand-dollar athletic scholarship from Elmhurst."

"Can he do that?" Carter asked.

"Sure. He can *promise*," I said. "But Elmhurst can't give athletic scholarships."

"Do you think Wisniewski will play for South Haven?" Chris said. "Their coach was trying to talk Mike into it the other day."

"Mike will play for us," I said. "He just has difficulty saying what he means. It's the source of some of Mike's problems."

"What are you gonna do?" Carter asked.

"Wait," I said. "Mike isn't gonna go play with a bunch of strangers when he can play with his best friends."

Alex kept jumping in and out of my lap. Finally, Mike sat down on the carpet and the little tricolor shelty crawled all over him. Mike rolled him over and scratched his stomach. "Alex, what is the matter with you?"

"Look at these uniforms." Carter held an athletic supply catalogue up. "They are diggity. I like the red and gray ones."

Wisser, Chris, and Carter began pouring over sports equipment catalogues my brother Jamie had sent. Carter's uncle was going to show him how to find and order the uniforms—it was a job the Bangor recreation program should have been doing.

Except for making the kids spend money to attend useless "coaching clinics" hosted by big-name college coaches, the Bangor coaches and athletic department didn't seem to care what happened to their student athletes during the summer.

"The teachers and coaches are sure different now than when I was working at school," Carter's grandmother said. "Rod Halstead and Marlon Howard would never just let the whole summer go by without checking on what their players were doing."

Now, nobody at the school will do anything unless they get paid. "Halstead and Howard built state championship teams," I said. "These new coaches don't do much even *when* they do get paid. They either have few skills or are so ambitious for personal success they don't want to spend time teaching and getting experience at the high school level. Sometimes I wonder if they like kids." I shook my head.

The boys were looking through the catalogues for the first and only real full uniforms they had ever had for Connie Mack. But the problem was still the same. We had no money and the uniforms were going to cost about seventy dollars apiece. The kids couldn't afford them. I would have to find the money.

I decided to take Carter's earlier advice and call on an old friend Tony Eicas. Tony and his wife, Ruth, lived in South Haven. During all the years he was plant manager of Adams' Electronics, Tony had lived in Bangor. He, my father, and other parents had raised money for sports projects when my brothers and I were at Bangor High School and Tony's daughter Roberta was a cheerleader.

Thirty-four years later Tony came through again. Within two weeks of asking, Tony and Ruth had collected and delivered enough money to buy fifteen uniforms.

Then Carter's mother called from Texas and offered to buy fitted Boston Red Sox hats for the whole team. The hats perfectly matched the uniforms. It was a nice thing to do.

In the past few years, Carter's mother began to take a more active interest in his sports activities in Bangor. Sports, especially baseball, gave them a common ground they badly needed. Sports gave Carter and his mother a framework in which to repair the damage she had done, heal old wounds, and rebuild their relationship, which grew healthier as the seasons passed. She came and visited him during basketball and both—high school and Connie Mack—baseball seasons. During her visits they grew closer and closer; she became the constant fan, taking pictures and making albums. Much was forgiven.

Also, Carter's sister, Holly, and her husband became followers of Bangor's athletic programs. They subscribed to the South Haven paper to keep track of Carter's progress. In the seventies Holly had been a Bangor Junior High School cheerleader. When we moved from Bangor, her fourteen-year-old world was devastated. She had had to rebuild her life in Wimberley, Texas.

I had felt guilty for a long time over forcing her to move away from the life she had loved in Bangor. But now, she was very happily married to a good man, and, if we hadn't moved, who knows how her life would have turned out??

29 ◇ Opening Day—Summer 1993

"WHAT'S THE MATTER, DAD?" Carter glanced over from the driver's seat. "Your back hurt?"

"Yeah." The pieces of lumbar disk rubbing against nerves still caused pain in my back, hamstring, and hip muscles. Needles and pins worked my left leg and foot.

"But that's not what's bothering me," I said. I shifted the pillow lower against my spine and rested my neck against the headrest. "I wish I was a better coach. I am actually sick to my stomach that we might not qualify for the State Tournament this year.''

"We'll be all right," Carter said. Near the Kalamazoo city limits, Carter turned off of M-43 and headed south on U.S. 131 toward Vicksburg. "Don't take it so serious. I'll still love you," Carter added. "I won't be able to hang out with you, but I'll still love you in my own way."

"I never got the team organized enough to even have one practice, we still don't have uniforms, and we are on our way to play the Maroons."

We were traveling to play our opening double-header of the season against the Kalamazoo Maroons. It was June 17, 1993.

Our uniforms were on order, but delivery was anybody's guess. So once again, we showed up in mismatched outfits.

Just south of Kalamazoo, Vicksburg High School provided the properly attired Maroons home field and the ground rules showed it. So did the umpires. Before the game ended, the home plate umpire threw Ben Finch out because Eric Finch had complained about a call. It seemed pointless to argue with the umpire that he had ejected the wrong twin. He seemed confused enough.

All the close calls seemed to go against us and some of the not-so-close ones.

According to the Maroons's ground rules, everything outside of our small dugout was in play and we could not keep anything outside the dugout, except the on-deck batter. We had to stay jammed in the claustrophobic hole in the ground, tripping on and stepping over bats, gloves, catching equipment, and other gear. Meanwhile, for the Maroons, the ground rules designated a roomy out-of-play area next to their dugout that was about sixty square feet. There the Maroons could put equipment, gloves, or just lounge around.

The Maroons stayed comfortable and cocky while we were wadded into the tiny, hot hole in the ground they called the visitors dugout.

That kind of mean-spirited, psyche-out head game angered me more than anything. The Maroons were lacking the sporting behavior that was prevalent in previous years. What was wrong with Hinga?

"Look at the scouts." Carter pointed toward the stands where several men with radar guns and notepads were sitting.

"The Maroons are undefeated," I said.

"Do you think any of the scouts are here to look at Wisniewski?" Carter asked.

"Probably." I looked at the men. "Since he blew away Jeter last year, I've gotten several calls about him from guys claiming to be college and pro scouts."

"Chris said a Dodger scout is here to watch that Sachs kid from Indiana. He's got a full ride at Western Michigan and is playing this summer with the Maroons."

"The Dodger scout is probably Dale McReynolds. He lives in Wisconsin. He called me about Wisniewski," I said. "Oh! I forgot to tell you. A scout from the Padres is coming to our home game against Coldwater. He saw you and Mike play in the high school regionals and is interested in both of you."

"Did he say 'both of us' or are you making that up so I'll feel good?" Carter said.

"I am repeating what he told me."

The game was a pitchers' duel between Wisniewski and Dennis Gest. First or second in the Maroons rotation, Gest had good speed and control. So did Mike, in addition to his god-awful knuckleball and nasty curve.

Before it was over, Hinga would have to bring in Pat Dunham, his other number one pitcher, to close the five-inning game. Hinga was obviously desperate, using his two top pitchers in one game to try and put us away. Wisniewski went the distance.

The game stayed 0–0 to the third inning. I noticed that Hinga was getting upset. He didn't seem to like the idea of the Maroons not just blowing us out immediately.

When Carter drove in the first run in the third inning to put us ahead, 1–0, Hinga lost it. Carter had had a good high school season and it had carried over into this first Connie Mack game against the Maroons.

As the game progressed, it had become more and more noticeable that some of the Maroons lacked the style, class, and grace the team had shown in previous seasons. Mike Hinga let his anger get the best of him. Even though the Maroons came back and tied the score, 1–1, in the bottom of the third, he never regained his composure. He began to yell and storm. He made cruel and cutting remarks to my players. His players seemed scared. He was obviously under pressure to win. I guess it was to make us pay for all the trouble we caused him last year.

It's an old saw that you humiliate your opponent early and you won't have to worry about him again. It just wasn't working out that way. The Maroons seemed to be embarrassing themselves. We never took anything that seriously. We took the first game into the final inning tied, 1–1.

The league rules stated that the first five-inning game of the doubleheader must end in the fifth inning, so a tie was quite possible. Hinga, though, did not want to settle for a tie and it was obvious that he would do just about anything to make certain the Maroons won the first game against us.

The longer the game remained tied, the worse Hinga behaved. It was easy to see the umpires were scared of him. But my back was aching and I was too drained by pain to argue calls. I smoked cigarettes to cause headaches that would make me forget my back, leg, and neck pain.

With two outs in the bottom of the fifth, I had repositioned my infield wrong and that had allowed a pop-up to drop in for a single. It should have been a simple third out and my mistake forced Wisniewski to have to face one more batter, Brad Block.

Nuke had Block down 0–2, when Mike let his fastball get up a little high and Block hit a long fly that barely cleared the Maroons shamefully short left-field fence.

I figured that short left-field fence was why the Maroons used the Vicksburg field. The winning home run would merely have been a long fly out at Bangor where the left-field line was 315 feet. The Maroons left-field fence was only 280.

In the second game, bottom of the second inning, Gary Gravatt made a spectacular play deep in the hole but was unable to make the throw in time. The Maroons hitter beat it by a step.

"A good shortstop would have made that play," Hinga, in the third base coaching box, was yelling loudly to Gary. "You couldn't play for my team."

"I wouldn't play for you," Gravatt replied. "You jerk."

"You tell 'em, Gary!" said Gravatt's father, who was dressed in a white T-shirt, jeans, and motorcycle boots and standing behind the backstop where he had overheard the dialogue. Hinga whirled and took several long strides toward the backstop.

"Why don't you shut up!" Hinga stormed, red-faced. "You . . . you fat . . . you fat beached whale!"

I knew it was going to be a long season. I was embarrassed for Mike and angry at the same time. Yelling at a kid's parent is not good form and way out of line. Yelling at Gary's dad was dangerous.

Something was certainly bothering Mike, but if he wasn't careful, he just might get aired-out with a deer rifle. Ugly things were going to happen; and the worst behavior would be exhibited by the adults: coaches, umpires, parents.

What I had told Carter driving to the game was coming to pass much faster than I had expected. I was not ready, physically or mentally, to handle it. Confrontations were to be avoided.

We lost the second game, 7–5, and with poor sportsmanship, the Maroons staff ignored my players and said nothing to me. Nobody shook hands. The Maroons picked up their equipment and avoided us until we left the field. *We* had lost both games. *They* were mad.

What was this all about? Was it was going to be a season of hard feelings? Was Hinga still mad about us knocking Kalamazoo Too out of the State District Tournament last year?

Returning to Bangor, we stopped for hamburgers in School-

craft, south of Kalamazoo. Everybody wanted to schedule a practice but nobody had the time. Obviously, practice would help.

"How's your back?" Carter asked, looking worried as he set
down his tray. "You want to go sit in the car? I'll bring your
food out to you."

"Maybe in a minute," I said. I studied the concern in his
face. "Hey, don't worry. It's not serious. I've just got something
pressing on a nerve."

"Oh, like a tumor?" he said. "I feel a lot better now."

"I don't have a tumor." I laughed, which shot pain from my
rib cage to my ankle. "Goddamnit, don't make me laugh."

"Here, let me set your food out." Carter waited on me, un-
wrapping my hamburger, setting out my fries, and putting the
straw in my milk shake.

"Hinga sure lost it out there when he thought we just might
take that first game." I sipped at the milk shake.

"He called Gary's dad a fat beached whale," Carter said.
"Could you believe he yelled at him?"

"I was surprised." I shook my head. "He has more class than
that. I wonder what was wrong with him? He didn't recover even
after they had won both games."

"Gary wanted to punch Hinga out for yelling at his dad,"
Carter said. "He would do it too. Remember last year?"

Last summer Gary Gravatt, who starred at nearby Gobles High
School, had played for us and led us to a win against Kalamazoo
Too. Gary made two double plays at shortstop, pitched two no-
hit innings in relief, and went four for five, including the winning home run that was fifty feet in the air when it went over
the fence at the 320 mark. After promising to be at our next
game against the Maroons, where he might well mean the difference between winning and losing, Gary went to a bar and got
drunk. He was busy punching holes in the Sheetrock wall of
the bar's rest room, when he finally misjudged his punch and
drove his fist smack into the two-by-four stud and broke his
hand.

Before this summer was over, Gary would break his foot in a

fight while kicking his opponent in the ribs. Gravatt fit right in with the boys from Bangor.

"I can't believe Hinga got so upset; that was tight," Carter said.

"You know," I said, changing the subject. "Nuke really wants to do what you tell him to do. He knows he has a chance to make it and has to control his head. He gets no help from the school."

I was caught in a peculiar bind—while trying to impress upon Mike Wisniewski that his baseball skills could lead to great opportunities in life, I kept agonizing over what Carter would decide about playing ball after high school. To me, playing after high school was dicey at best. I had painted myself into a philosophical corner and it was difficult for me to step back and look objectively at that subject for Carter. It made for some peculiar situations, like the time we had dinner with Bears coach Mike Ditka in 1988.

Carter was still in junior high school and Mike had invited Carter and me in from Michigan for dinner with him and his wife at his downtown Chicago restaurant. The Bears had already won a Super Bowl and were still definite contenders. Ditka was a superstar in Chicago and the NFL. Carter had been around famous people most of his life and was generally unimpressed. But Mike Ditka had an aura about him that held even Carter in thrall. I held Ditka in high regard myself.

During the course of dinner, Carter seldom took his eyes off Ditka as people came by to pay homage in a never-ending stream.

Finally, as we finished eating, Mike turned to Carter. "Carter, what sports do you play?" he asked.

"I play baseball and"—Carter held his hands up for inspection—"I am a real good receiver in football."

He was. I discouraged his playing. But when he played sandlot he could catch the ball. When he reached high school, the strain between us was great. Each fall was agony, as he had to sit in the stadium and watch his friends play, doubly pained with the knowledge that he possessed the skills to play the game well. His arguments were impassioned and respectful, as every year he tried to convince me that he wanted and needed to play football.

"My dad doesn't want me to play football," Carter said, flexing his fingers as he talked to Ditka. "It's terrible not being able to play with all my friends."

Ditka paused, gathering his thoughts. Carter stared, still mesmerized.

"You know, Carter," Ditka said finally. "Football's okay. But a guy like you ought to be practicing sports like golf and tennis. Those are sports you can play your whole life long."

Ditka had just repeated, nearly verbatim, what I had been repeating like a mantra for months whenever Carter brought up his desire to play football.

Carter's jaw dropped. The gleam left his eye, replaced by confusion, then irritation. Carter looked back and forth from Mike's face to mine in stunned silence.

"But . . . but . . . you're just like my dad," Carter said finally.

In an instant, Ditka was reduced from high in Carter's pantheon of gods to something resembling a . . . a parent. "You both played football and now you say I can't do it. That's not fair."

"But, Carter," I added, "we're just trying to show you the alternatives . . . the other sports. You're so good in baseball and basketball. And I know if you tried tennis and golf you'd be good in those sports."

"It's not fair," Carter said, looking down at his plate. He continued to flex his fingers. "You both played football."

Mike's wife, Diana, looked over at Mike, then at me.

"He's got ya." She smiled. She was right. He had me. Years later, he still had me.

30 ◇ Coaches

It's a decadent profession . . . I go back to the days when we were educators. . . . Now, we are entertainers . . . we are Ringling Brothers directors.

—BEN JOBE, basketball coach, Southern University

"YOU KNOW . . ." CARTER WAS driving again west of Kalamazoo on M-43 heading toward Bangor. He glanced at me out of the corner of his eye. "I have to go to varsity basketball camp at Ohio State next week. We'll be gone until Friday."

"Damn, I forgot. I hate all these off-season camps. They are ruining high school sports," I said. "Spring and summer are for baseball. Fall is for football. Winter is for basketball."

I was mad because I would miss Carter off the field and on the field. This year with my back still blown, I had come to depend on Carter to do everything. He had been my arms, legs, eyes, ears, and brain for the last several weeks.

Also, this was our last summer together and I was husbanding each moment desperately. Now, this jerk basketball coach was taking Carter off to Ohio State and wasting four days out of the heart of our time together.

The basketball camp was a sudden reminder of my fragility. Carter going to Columbus, Ohio, for a week punctured the delicate membrane of sentience that held back the accumulated years of woe and mistrust, filling me with separation anxiety.

"How can you abandon me at such a difficult time?" I whined. "The man who has been both father and mother to you."

"Breast-feed me and then we'll talk," Carter said. "Meanwhile, put Eric Finch at second for the next game. He went a whole high school season at second without a fielding error."

By the time Carter had driven us back to Bangor from Vicksburg, my back had gone into deep spasm. I could not straighten up. Carter had to help me from the car into the house.

I told Carter, Chris Christian, and Mike Wisniewski that I felt our victory was measured by how nuts Hinga went even after they had won both games. "We have a moral victory," I said as I eased down on my side and drew up my right knee to ease the tightness in my back.

"How does that figure in the standings?" Carter frowned and pulled off his jersey. "We're still 0–2. Do we get more of those mysterious points for a tie or a moral victory?"

"You boys put your dirty clothes in the washing machine," Carter's grandmother said. "I'll fix you sandwiches and then start a load of wash tonight. I'll have your stuff nice and clean for your next game. It feels good to put on clean clothes."

It was eleven P.M. and Carter's eighty-year-old grandmother, who had a congestive heart, was going to fix sandwiches for however many of the players stopped by and then wash all their uniforms. Thirty-four years earlier, she had done the very same things for my two brothers, me, and all our teammates. She would continue to take care of the kids all summer long. She washed their clothes, fed them, and made up extra beds, often until well after midnight following games.

"When do we get our uniforms?" Wisniewski asked.

"Probably in a couple weeks," I said. "Carter's uncle has ordered them for us."

"Great," Carter said. "We can have our names put on the jerseys at that place in Paw Paw."

"It will only cost about a dollar a letter," Chris said.

"That will cost Wisniewski a fortune," Carter said.

Wisniewski blushed, his full cheeks turning bright red.

"You should just put 'Nuke' on your jersey," I offered.

A couple weeks later when the uniforms arrived Wisniewski did put a nickname on the back, but it wasn't "Nuke," it was "Whiz." When I saw it I wondered if he realized the heckling he would get from the Maroons bench jockeys.

The boys stripped down, took showers, put on clean clothes,

and ate the sandwiches Carter's grandmother had made. Then they decided to drive over to Paw Paw and cruise the Taco Bell.

"Dad? How 'bout some snaps?" Carter was standing over me, showered and smelling fresh. His hair was slicked back.

"Snaps?" I frowned at him.

"Ducats, green, wood, you know, snaps." Carter held out his hand. "I need gas, I've only got a half clip for my nine millie, plus money for the drugs, girls, and the motel rooms."

"Carter!" His grandmother snapped at him. "Don't even joke about stuff like that."

"Who's joking, Granny? It's a jungle out there." Carter grinned and hugged his grandmother.

"My snaps are in my coat pocket in the hall, Vanilla Ice." When I turned and tried to stretch my lower back, something in my neck ground and popped.

The boys left for Paw Paw. Carter's grandmother had fed them, cleaned up the kitchen and bathroom after they left, then washed the dirty towels and game clothes. Finally she climbed the steep stairs to the upstairs bedrooms and made up their beds for when they returned from Paw Paw to sleep.

"It's always good to get into a nice, clean bed at night," she said after she hobbled over on her arthritic legs and sat next to me. "My fingers ache and . . . whew! I'm tired."

"I wonder why."

I lay on my side and pondered exactly what it was the Great Depression had done to people like my mother that kept them from ever sitting still for more than half an hour before getting up to wash, sweep, vacuum, or dust.

◇

"Are you going to let me pitch this summer?" Carter asked the next day. "I've really been working on my curve. It is nasty."

I hesitated before replying. He knew why I didn't want him to pitch. I was afraid he would catch a line drive right back in the face.

"I pitched in Babe Ruth and won a lot of games," Carter said. "I was good. Come on, give me a chance."

He was telling the truth. He had been a good pitcher with speed and control. I was screwing him again. But each pitch he threw in Babe Ruth had filled me with dread.

"If you weren't going to Ohio State," I said, "you could pitch next week against Gull Lake or RATHCO." It was an easy thing to say.

"Yeah." Carter glanced sideways at me. "Right."

It was not like I was fooling him.

"When your uncles and I were in school, summer camps like that were illegal." Suddenly, an illogical, free-floating anger had slipped its leash. "Now, everybody acts like high school is just early training for the NBA. Who appointed a goddamn hamburger franchise as the keeper of the flame for high school basketball?"

"What are you talking about?" Carter's eyes widened. He had seen me completely lose touch before.

"At your age," I replied, "sports aren't supposed to be a major career move. Sports are to teach people character so they learn to survive in the world. It is not about the McDonald's All-American High School Team and Nike's All-Star Camp in Las Vegas. That's business. Dirty business. I've never seen a business create good people. Business takes good people and eats them."

"Dad?" Carter frowned and shook his head. "Hey, chill."

"Sorry." I tried to calm down. "But the real sports lessons are about failure, learning how to deal with it and recover. Baseball especially is about failure. You fail six out of ten times at the plate and you are a major star."

"I know, Dad. We've had this conversation before." Carter sighed. "We are all doomed to fail and—"

"So?" I cut him off. "I can't be thinking up new stuff every day. I just think summer camps are ninety percent swindle. I'm sick of college coaches cashing in on their schools, their players, and their names and pretending there isn't anything slightly smelly about the whole deal. Money turns bad fast and stinks up sports.''

"I don't know why the coach chose Ohio State.'' Carter shifted gears and tried to steer me away from the subject. "It's a long drive and the other schools in this camp are supposed to be mac daddy teams. Teams with mad skills and six-eight point guards. We won't do well.''

"I'll tell you why you're going,'' I said. "So your idiot coach can hang around Randy Ayres and other coaches trying to net-work his way to success. Willy Loman as a basketball coach.''

Before Carter left, we sat down with Mike Wisser to plot out the next week's games and rosters. Carter would be gone and Chris Christian had to miss the RATHCO game to work at the video store. And, as usual, the rest of the team planned to arrive at the last possible minute. We needed to pick up a couple more players.

"Wisniewski and I can catch for Chris,'' Mike Wisser said.

Both Mikes were excellent catchers with strong arms.

"You better pitch Brian Seymour against Gull Lake,'' Carter continued. "Because the next day we got Kalamazoo Too at Bangor and the day after we play RATHCO in Kalamazoo. Greg Grosvenor from Decatur will come next week,'' Carter added. "He can pitch. If we can get Mike Fusco from Decatur too, you should have enough players until I get back. Then, put me in the pitching rotation. I am telling you I've got a nasty curve.''

I nodded but didn't answer.

Eventually, I did let Carter pitch. One game against KTOO at the end of the season. he threw fine but quickly tired because I hadn't encouraged him to keep his arm in shape.

Later in high school he would go 3–0, shutting out Gobles for five innings and striking out thirteen against Paw Paw. He still had the good control he had showed in Little League and Babe Ruth, when I wouldn't let him throw breaking stuff. And now, he *really did* have a nasty curve. That ball started high and out-side, then curved, dropped, and broke clear across into the dirt on the other side of the plate.

After he had won constantly as a pitcher for me in three years of Little League and Babe Ruth, I used him only once during all the time I was so desperate for pitchers in Connie Mack. It's hard to explain my reasoning sometimes. In the seventies I was convinced that *Skylab* was going to fall on me.

◇

The next morning Carter drove over to the high school to hunt down the recreation director and make certain the field would be ready for the Gull Lake and Kalamazoo Too games. When he returned, he sat down on the couch. I was flat on the floor, working the cramps out of my lower back. "Nobody knows what is going on down there," he said, his voice tense. "The high school wrestling coach was supposed to be in charge of the recreation program. But he quit yesterday."

"I'll miss you." I ran my hands up and down Carter's sides and could feel every rib. He was so thin. Happily, he had had no repetitions of the irregular heartbeat in over a year.

"Don't worry, Dad. I'll work it out before I go," said Carter, playing father to the man. "You just rest your back."

"Thanks, but what I mean is I will really miss you." I pulled him down across my chest and nuzzled into the back of his neck.

"Oh, I'll miss you too." He sat up and looked at me. "I love you, Dad." Leaning back down, he hugged me.

"Love you, bub." I kneaded at the knotted muscles in his back and neck. He had been getting them when he was tense since he was six years old. When the divorce was going full blast, I would find knots in his back and neck the size of golf balls. Sometimes it would take me hours to massage and work the spasms out of his skeletal muscles. There were days he was tense as a bowstring.

"It'll be okay." He sat back and patted my cheek. "I'm kind of excited to see St. John's Arena at Ohio State."

"Did I ever tell you I played my last college basketball game in St. John's Arena?" I grabbed his arm because I knew he would try and run as soon as I started this story. "The Big Ten title was on the line when I took a long long long jump shot with five seconds left for the win. . . ."

"Yeah, Dad, you told me." He tried to stand and I pulled him back down.

"Ohio State had never lost a game at St. John's, and if we beat them it put Cazzie Russell and Michigan in the NCAA Tournament . . ." I was relentless.

"You told me," said Carter, trying to wriggle free as I held him down. "You told me a million times."

"I was shooting from so far downtown a city bus nearly hit me." I had him pinned. He fought to get loose.

Carter finally pulled free and jumped away from me.

"Dad, please, no more of your Nam stories."

"So, I told you, huh? It was a great story."

"You told me." Carter walked over to the coffee table and picked up the *Kalamazoo Gazette*.

"Did you see the article in here about Derek Jeter?" He turned quickly to the sports section.

"He's playing Double A in the Yankee farm system." Carter held up the paper. "I'm telling you, Dad, Jeter is going to the major leagues. He is great."

Carter's face lit up. He was actually happy for Derek Jeter. I envied him the purity he still felt for sports. He had had some of the worst coaches, including me, and been dealt disappointing setbacks. Since junior high only a couple of his coaches knew anything about their sports. The rest were unskilled, lacked any real knowledge, could not teach fundamentals or technique, and thought coaching talent was ranked on a decibel scale.

Yet, Carter still loved sports. He loved to play. He loved to watch. He loved to talk about sports and the players. There was an unconditional appreciation of skill that filled him and allowed him to enjoy all aspects of all sports.

My coaches had been the best of their time and place. The best programs and systems of championship caliber. And, finally, we won. We were winners.

Yet, Carter truly appreciated sports and I shied away. I was conflicted; and one thing seemed certain: Carter was right. His view was positive, optimistic, and flowed freely toward generosity and virtue. He was growing and learning.

I was out of sync. My view was angry, dark, and depressing, cutting short any real appreciation of skill, keeping me from fully enjoying the beauty of athletics, stunting my growth.

All that evening and night, Carter's grandmother carefully packed his bags while Carter went out with Mike Wisser and Chris Christian to South Haven. They would cruise along the Lake Michigan beach. The huge mansions that had housed the hundreds of Jewish families all those summers ago were gone, replaced by condos filled with aging yuppies. Instead of finned and chromed Detroit iron, the streets were now lined with slick, fuel-injected computer-driven imports. I worried about Carter in South Haven.

When my brothers and I had spent our summers cruising South Haven, at worst an evening had ended up in a small scrap with some South Haven kids over girls. The usual weapons were harsh language. Sometimes an actual fight would break out for about one or two punches, then everybody was satisfied that the evening hadn't been a total waste of time.

Now, South Haven was cashing in on the tourism boom, becoming a resort town of a totally different nature. It wasn't about the beauty of the lakeshore and the farm country. It was all about money. Expensive lakeside homes sat perilously close to the eroding cliffs overlooking Lake Michigan, millions of dollars in boats docked in marinas on the Black River. There were boat slips adjoining expensive condominiums.

Thirty years ago, my brothers and our friends all hung out at the Zephyr Drive Inn on the edge of town with its carhops and girls in Daddy's T Bird. Now, underage kids tried to slip into the dozens of bars with names like Captain Nemo's, Captain Lou's, and Clementine's.

The town boomed in the summer. It had gone from a sleepy summer resort to fast-track real estate speculation and a cash trade in liquor licenses and all the corruption that entails. There was an underworld: robbery, drugs, guns, real estate, and fountain pens.

Big money scams like strip malls and lakefront property. And, making it worse, South Haven was only twenty minutes off of I-94, the fast lane from Detroit to Chicago. The street gangs from both cities were expanding along the Interstate. Turf wars were coming to town. There were armed robberies and drive-bys.

I breathed easier when the boys returned from South Haven early and played basketball late into the night. Early Sunday morning, Carter was off to basketball camp and I was on my own.

I was lonely by noon.

31 ◇ Gull Lake

WITH CARTER GONE, THE first hurdle was the Monday doubleheader against Gull Lake in Bangor. Gull Lake was a big Class A/B school on the east side of Kalamazoo. They arrived about an hour before game time and began warming up in the outfield.

"Where's my kid?" asked Mike Wisser's father, Jim, stepping down in the dugout.

"The Finch twins drove to Upjohn's to pick him up from work," I said. "What's Mike going to do about college?"

"He's going to Wabash in Indiana." Jim smiled. "Mike has a full ride academically and the coaches are telling him how much they want him to come there," Jim continued. "He wants to play baseball and basketball and both coaches are telling him he will step right in and play."

"Now, the only question is, are they telling Mike the truth," I said.

"Well, Wabash has a pretty good reputation for academics." Jim nodded. He was no fool.

"It is their coaches' reputation for honesty that I am wondering about."

"You gotta believe somebody or you go crazy."

"That was an operative phrase in Hollywood," I said. "I was

hoping I would never hear it in this dugout. Just remind Mike, a winner is simply the guy who gets back up one more time than he gets knocked down. Ninety percent of life is just showing up."

In the parking lot, Steve Leonard had just pulled in and was changing clothes. A moment later, the twins drove up with Mike Wisser. We had enough players, and over fifteen minutes to spare.

We won without much difficulty. The Gull Lake coach was more concerned with developing his younger players than winning. He was a nice guy.

Brian Seymour pitched. He hadn't pitched since the previous spring and was set to quit baseball altogether, until Carter talked him into playing Connie Mack. Brian pitched well and it showed in his face. Being a winning pitcher can put a lot back into your life.

Up in the parking lot after the game, Brian's mother, Debbie, pulled up beside me in her station wagon. "I just wanted to thank you," Debbie said. "It meant so much to Brian to pitch today. He has been so disappointed. He was ready to quit."

"He's put in too many long summer nights to quit now," I said.

"Well, I just wanted you to know how much Greg and I appreciated Carter talking him into playing this summer." She drove off.

I leaned against the car and let the last of the butterflies finally land and my nerves calm down. This was the best time. After the kids won and I got to watch how pleased they were with themselves. They had bumped up their self-esteem and come that much closer to maturity.

Today had been a bonus. A parent had thanked me for letting her kid do what he was capable of doing. I had done nothing but get out of the kid's way and his mother thanked me for it.

It would have been perfect had Carter been there. I missed him. Talking over the game with Carter was what I looked forward to most of all. He would have done well today and I missed not getting to watch him perform. It made me angry. By taking the varsity basketball team off to Ohio State, Carter's coach had stolen five days and six baseball games from our last summer.

32 ◇ The Phone Call

THE PHONE RANG AS I stepped through the door. Carter was calling from Columbus. "Did we win?" he asked.

I gave him a quick rundown on the game's highlights.

"I wish I could have been there," he said. "This camp sucks. One team has a six-nine point guard. All we do is scrimmage and get hammered. I finally know the meaning of 'intimidation.' "

"We got Kalamazoo Too here tomorrow," I said.

"I know," Carter responded. "We can't lose to them. Did you move Eric Finch to second like I told you?"

"Yeah, he made several good plays. Wisniewski worked behind the plate and hit an inside-the-park home run. It went so high in the air, he was at third base by the time it came down."

Carter laughed. "How did Brian do?"

"He got a win and seemed happy about it. You could have pitched the second game."

"Yeah, you say that when I'm three hundred miles away. Any of the guys there now?" Carter asked.

"Nope, the moment you left town the phone quit ringing and nobody stopped by."

"Don't worry, I'll be back Thursday night. Love you."

I told him to take care of himself and that I loved him too.

Once I was off the phone, it began: that lonely feeling that had haunted me since Carter was first wrenched away by the gunmen. The irrational fear of losing him was never far from mind. I told myself over and over that there was nothing I could do to protect him or myself. But, the fears just grew.

"Was that Carter?" his grandmother called to me.

"Yeah," I said, pushing myself out of the chair and walking into the front room to talk with her. "He says the basketball camp is awful." I slumped down on the sofa bed. "I can't stand that coach. He is too young to be a head coach."

"You better be careful saying that." My mother was sitting in her favorite chair, sewing. "You made the high school principal really mad when you said he was 'just too young to understand.' "

"Hah. A high school principal so stupid I couldn't insult him." I bent to stretch my back. "I can't deal with those people at the school."

After his freshman year in high school Carter had told me not to go to school when he was having problems. "Just stay away, unless they call you down there," Carter had said. "You just go crazy and they take it out on me."

"I am not going crazy when I disagree with the principal or the athletic director over the way they treat you," I had argued.

"Believe me, I can handle those guys better than you," Carter had insisted, and he won the argument.

"You are only causing Carter trouble when you go down there and throw a fit," his grandmother cautioned. "So leave Carter's basketball coach alone."

"I do leave him alone, except for the one time that son of a bitch grabbed Carter and was swearing at him." I tried to defend myself. "It just drives me nuts that he really believes his life is a mixture of *Hoosiers* and Bobby Knight."

"Didn't you know him?" My mother never looked up from her hand sewing. She was repairing Carter's sweatshirt.

"Who?" I eased myself prone on the couch. "Bobby Knight? He was playing at Ohio State when I was at Michigan State. But I never paid attention to him until he called the Puerto Rican woman's basketball team 'a bunch of whores.' "

"No, not Bobby Knight," said Carter's grandmother, looking up from the sweatshirt. "The guy in *Hoosiers*. That Hooper, the actor?"

"Hopper?" I turned on my side. "Dennis Hopper? Yeah, I know Dennis. We were in Durango for seven months in 1971–72, trying

to see who could do the most drugs. It was while I was writing
North Dallas Forty."

"Oh, Peter!" My mother looked back down at her sewing.
"Quit talking like that. You didn't really take drugs?"

"Apparently, I didn't take enough. Dennis won. That's why
he gets to do the Nike commercials. It's weird watching him get
paid by Nike to behave the same way he did in Durango." The
aching was settling bone deep in my legs and back.

"Was he crazy?" My mother never looked up.

"We were all crazy. It was the movies," I said. "Dennis was
fascinating. He's like Nolte, Willie Nelson, and Kenny Rogers.
I've known them a long time and they've survived some awful
stuff."

"Have you talked to Nolte lately?"

"Not in over a year," I replied. "Not since *People* magazine
picked him as the Sexiest Man Alive."

I recalled a six-two, forty-year-old, slightly debilitated Nolte,
chasing a two-six, three-year-old Carter up and down the corri-
dors of the Westwood Marquis while I worked on the next day's
Blue Pages for *North Dallas Forty,* both wearing nothing but their
Jockeys. "Yeah. Nick has always been the sexiest man in Hollywood. Who else is there? Tom Cruise? He's three feet tall."

"I always liked that boy," my mother said. "Even before you
knew him. I thought he was wonderful in *Rich Man, Poor Man.*"

"He's a star and he has survived." A sudden back pain
brought me back to the real subject at hand. "Survival is the real
game. The last one to die wins. I coulda been a contender, Ma."

"Get a haircut. It will make you feel a lot better," she said. It
was her solution to all my complaints.

"I miss Carter," I whined.

She stopped sewing and looked at me over the tops of her
glasses. "You better start getting used to it," she said. "Can you
imagine what it was like for your father?"

"What?" I stretched out on the couch and groaned.

"You three boys," she continued. "In 1958 Charlie and you

were still in high school and Jamie was in eighth grade. This house was like Grand Central Station. Your dad loved it.''

"It was pretty incredible," I agreed. "After a game there might be twenty people here, parents and kids, players and cheerleaders.''

"Your father said it was the best time of his life." My mother stared out the side window at the American Legion Hall, converted from the original Sacred Heart Church.

"By March 1960 we were chasing a state title in basketball," I said. "An amazing time, there was nothing like it again.''

"All you kids were here every day." My mother didn't seem to hear what I had said. "Then, Charlie gets married, you go off to Michigan State. Two years later, Jamie goes even farther to Central Michigan . . .''

I waited a moment for her to finish. She was silent. I looked over and saw she had removed her glasses and was wiping tears from her eyes. They had streaked her face. Her nose was running.

"Oh damnit," she said quietly as she wadded up the Kleenex and wiped her nose. "You boys and your friends were so much of his life. He never really quite handled how fast you guys grew and were just suddenly gone.''

I looked at the darkened outside window beside the sofa and my father's face reflected back at me.

"Carter is going to grow up and leave." She was back at work on Carter's sweatshirt. "And once he is gone, there is very little you can do.''

"Yeah, I know," I said. "I know he is going. I don't know how the hell I am going to deal with it.''

"You better start thinking about it.''

"I have been thinking about it. Sometimes all I do is think about how fast time is passing. How my attempts to prepare for Carter's future are so feeble.''

"There . . . that ought to last about two weeks." She held up the sweatshirt.

"One thing I do know," I said. "Right now the team needs Carter back."

Carter's importance to the team was especially apparent in his absence. He held the team together with his energy, love, and sense of responsibility. His teammates returned that love openly and genuinely. It was a rare thing to see young men express such depth of feeling for each other. It probably wouldn't last, few things in life did. But it was inspiring as long as it did. Those kids still just loved to play the game together. They were still a "team" in the purest sense—each wanted victory for the others.

Every day, after they got off work, if we didn't have a game scheduled, they went to the batting cages or organized a pickup game against anybody they could find.

One of the legendary Bangor pickup games took place on an early-summer afternoon just before we started the Connie Mack season. Carter, Chris Christian, Wisniewski, Wisser, and Steve Leonard were practicing hitting down at the ballpark when two battered old pickup trucks pulled up and thirty Mexican migrant workers piled out.

"They were nice guys, Dad. You should have seen it," Carter told me later. "About half of them were barefoot. They wanted to play a baseball game."

"So, it was us against them." Carter laughed at his own recollections. "Thirty guys . . . the outfield was full. They were lined up from fence to fence. There was not one open place to hit. We had a great time."

"What kind of players were they?"

"Some of them were pretty good. They didn't have any equipment and couldn't believe that we had so many bats and balls and gloves," Carter replied. "We loaned all the gloves we had, a few of them had their own, and the rest played bare-handed or would try and catch the ball in their hats."

"When we were playing," Carter said, "I got to looking around at just how bizarre the whole thing looked and all I could think was 'where else would this happen but Bangor?' "

Lying on the couch, lonely and tired from the Gull Lake game, recalling Carter's story, I suddenly had to fight to keep from being overwhelmed by depression. For over ten years, terrors and remorse would emerge from the jungle of my mind and have me in a death struggle, fighting for my sanity. My subconscious was a triple-canopy rain forest with all the trails mined. Negotiating this wilderness was exhausting. So many mistakes. So much waste. In my life, I had achieved a lot by the time Carter was six years old. Then, my ex-wife hired the lawyers who called in snake and napalm on me. What dreams I had for my family were blown away.

All that was left was scorched earth.

Now, I crept through life. Long-term thinking was useless, I had to make my life up as I went along. Day after day, I woke scared and began reassembling my reality all over again. Each day I seemed to start off further behind than the day before. I had learned life's hardest lesson; a man controls nothing, not even his own family. Especially not his own family.

Years had passed and Carter grew and changed. He was becoming an intelligent and mannerly young man. He had an unlimited future, if I didn't become a burden and a hindrance. He was smart and a quick study. He'd do fine.

I was growing old and desperate to give some grace and meaning to my aging. For me, it was too late to live fast, die young, and leave a good-looking corpse. I had chosen not to do that after my experience in Hollywood. Yet, I never pictured myself in the future, next year or next week. I wasn't there.

During summer baseball, I could lose myself in the moment and come to life again. But, so many of those baseball moments were already gone and this last summer was coming rapidly to an end.

33 ◇ No Bozos on This Bus

AFTER TAKING TWO FROM Gull Lake, we needed to sweep Kalamazoo Too and RATHCO to make up for our two losses to the Maroons. This would move us to 6–2 in the standings. The way things were playing out, it looked like we would be battling the Maroons, Kalamazoo Too, and possibly Dave Martin's excellent Coldwater team for the tournament seeds allotted to our league.

"But," Dave Martin said to me on the phone, "if winning the division is what decides, what is the point system about?"

"Getting a straight answer out of Hinga is like trying to nail Jell-O to the wall," I replied. "I like the guy, but he definitely has his own agenda. I can't shake the feeling that he absolutely hates to lose to Bangor."

"Your guys are good." Dave laughed. "But, you certainly don't behave or dress the way Hinga thinks class players should."

"We should have uniforms for our next game against the Maroons. But that doesn't guarantee the kids will wear them right side out."

Tuesday, Greg Grosvenor arrived. The previous year, Greg had played for the Maroons and Kalamazoo Too. He was a good third baseman/pitcher with a good bat.

Chet Slazek, my friend and high school teammate, brought his two young boys, Matt and Joe, down to the game. Chet was a good fundamental pitching coach. He would offer to help Mike.

Chet had played football, basketball, and baseball in high school. Excelling in baseball, he was offered a contract from Pittsburgh in 1960 to play in one of the old C leagues. Instead, he went to Central Michigan University and roomed with my younger brother, Jamie. He graduated in time to be sent to Vietnam as a sergeant in the artillery. Chet was sent to a fire base in the central highlands with five American noncoms and a lieutenant. Guarded by Montagnards, they were under fire every day for six months and overrun twice.

We had both returned to Bangor in the early seventies. Chet was back from the ugly Asian war and I was recovering from success in the fast lane. Spending long, quiet winter nights drinking coffee and comparing close calls, we slowly talked each other back into the world.

"What a beautiful day," Chet said as we walked from the parking lot. "A good day to be alive and perfect for baseball."

"I hope everybody plays well," I said. "They can all go home feeling good about themselves."

Mike Wisniewski was pitching the first five-inning game and by the bottom of the third had built a comfortable 3–1 lead.

My back was still bad. The spasms and bone-deep ache the length of my left leg kept me confined to a lawn chair in the dugout. Chet was coaching third. Carter was gone. I didn't notice the trouble between Mike and his girl until it was too late. She had shown up just as the game began. Soon they were fighting and arguing behind the dugout between innings. By the fourth inning, Wisniewski went to pieces and gave up two runs to tie the game. In the fifth, he had two men on before the game ended with a groundout to Mike Wisser at first base. We were lucky to escape with a tie.

Having sufficiently tortured and driven my number one pitcher to the brink of insanity, the girl left before the second game. By the bottom of the fifth, Mike had recovered enough to hit a long double to drive in the tying and winning runs.

After the games, I reminded everybody that we played RATHCO the next day in Kalamazoo and had exactly nine players. We could not afford two forfeits after two losses to the Maroons and the tie with Kalamazoo Too. We had gotten off to a shaky start.

The players began to pick up equipment and fill the ball bags.

"Pete," Wisniewski spoke in his high-pitched Chicago accent. "I can't come to the game tomorrow. I gotta go to ... I ... ah." He dropped his eyes and stared at the ground. He wouldn't look at me. The others continued packing up our bats and gear.

"Mike. We only got nine players." I felt sorry for him. I felt sorry for me.

"I forgot that I gotta go to a wedding in Chicago," he said in a rush—a train roaring out of tunnel. He glanced up at me.

"We won't have enough ..." I caught myself and stopped. The strain was obvious in his face. He didn't need me guilt-tripping him. "Mike, get your life straight. That's more important."

"Thanks, Pete." Wisniewski quickly turned and walked away, already scurrying for that dark place where he hid from the confusions and terrors of his real life. At times, he was under so much stress, Mike literally could not calm his mind long enough to process his life experience as it was happening.

In Dallas, Bobby Hayes had been like that. Of course, he was a black man playing for the Cowboys in the sixties, when the apartments across from the Dallas Cowboys practice field did not rent to "coloreds."

Nuke and Bobby Hayes showed the same signs of constant crisis. Bobby handled it and became a star.

◇

Carter was gone four days and the team had fallen apart.

The day of the RATHCO game, Ben and Eric Finch were at my office working the phones trying to find two more bodies. Talent did not matter. Only seven players were ready to leave for Kalamazoo and the RATHCO game. Shaun Eisner could not make the 5:30 start time for the first game of the doubleheader. We could not afford to forfeit more games.

"I am going downtown," Eric said. "I'll see who I can find out on the streets."

In fifteen minutes Eric returned with Shane Wood. Shane had been a fine basketball player, until the idiot coach had driven him and six other good players off. Then Shane quit school. Unfortunately, Shane's talents did not include baseball and he was left-handed. We could not find him a glove. With Shane was another kid who would go to the game but didn't want to play.

"I ain't playing," he said. "I don't want to get hit."

"You gotta play," Eric pleaded.

"Come on, we need you," Ben added.

"I don't wanna play. I'll get hit in the head for sure when I'm up at bat." He seemed like he had taken one too many to the head already.

"You won't have to bat," I said. "We'll just take the out. You can sit in the dugout safe and sound."

"I could get hit out in the field."

"I'll put you deep in right field," I offered. "They hit into right, you wait until the ball stops rolling then pick it up and throw it back."

The kid frowned and looked around at the Finch twins and Shane Wood. Shane was trying a fielder's mitt on the wrong hand without much success.

"Okay," the kid finally agreed.

"Let's go. We're late," I said.

Halfway to Kalamazoo, Ben and Eric remembered they had left their gloves at my office. I was sweating from stress as I drove east. Hopefully our ending would be better than our beginning.

Two more games, I thought. Two more games and Carter will be back to handle all this.

By game time at the Kalamazoo Central baseball field, my back was cramping all the way from the nape of my neck to the back of my knees. The Finch twins found two old gloves of Carter's in the equipment bag. That just left Shane and the kid in right field as problems to be solved.

During infield practice, Kalamazoo Too looked young but well coached and they definitely had their minds on the game.

We took the field in the bottom of the first. Shane Wood was in left field wearing his fielder's glove on the wrong hand and the other kid in right field refused to touch any balls that were moving. Brian Seymour pitched well, retiring the first three batters. Both teams were scoreless going into the bottom of the second. Then Greg Grosvenor showed up and replaced the kid in right who strolled smiling to the safety of the dugout.

"Whew," he said, sitting next to me. "That was close. I was sure they were going to hit a ball at me anytime."

"Yeah." I nodded. "it is pretty scary out there without even worrying about the snakes."

"Snakes!" He whipped his head around and stared at me. "There are snakes out there? You coulda warned me."

In the bottom of the second, Brian Seymour beaned a KTOO batter. Unable to recover from the fear that he might have injured another player, Brian walked three and gave up three hits. RATHCO scored seven runs in the second.

Shaun Eisner arrived and replaced Shane Wood. Now we had a complete team. Unfortunately, RATHCO had scored another run and we were eight runs behind in the top of the third.

Eight to zip, the game half over. Goddamn five-inning games.

Mike Wisser was catching and had shouldered the role of leader single-handedly since we were missing Carter, Chris Christian, and Mike Wisniewski. Soaked with sweat, Mike already looked exhausted from working all day at the Upjohn Company. He had caught only two innings and had at least eight more to go, but Wisser pushed the other kids to work and they responded.

But despite a late-inning rally, we lost, 8–7. In five-inning games, all rallies are late-inning rallies.

In the second game, we beat RATHCO, 5–1.

The team had done well, despite Carter being gone, Wisniewski having girl trouble, and Christian missing to work. Against Gull Lake, Kalamazoo Too, and RATHCO, they had won four, lost one, and tied one. I was proud of them.

34 ◇ Uniforms

CARTER WAS BACK FROM Ohio State.

The next day the baseball uniforms arrived and in less than half an hour, Mike Wisser, Eric and Ben Finch, and Chris Christian were over checking them out. Steve Leonard and Carter had already torn open the boxes and pulled out the uniforms. They acted like kids at Christmas. It was hard to think of them as young men, soon to go out in the real world.

Was Carter really ever small enough for me to have carried around in my arms or on my shoulders with his chubby little legs straddling my neck? How much time had passed? How much was left?

"These are fiiiine, Dad!" Carter said, pulling on jersey number eight. "Whattaya think? Am I beyond diggity or what? We're going to Paw Paw right now and getting our names put on the backs of our jerseys."

"Carter," said his grandmother, who had been watching the kids dig through the boxes for shirts and pants. "All of those pants look too big. Let me look at yours."

She was right. All the pants were extra large and much too big at the waist for most of the kids.

"Let me measure each one of you," she said. "Then leave the pants here for me to sew while you go to Paw Paw." Arthritic fingers and all, it took her only three days to tailor the pants to fit each player.

We won the two doubleheaders against Colon and Paw Paw in Bangor. Carter went four for ten with two doubles. He was hitting hard and playing a good center field. It was good to have him back. The games took on special meaning again.

In the second game against Colon, Wisniewski got thirteen strikeouts in five innings. Mike Fusco from Decatur had joined us in the first game and moved in at shortstop to replace the injured Gary Gravatt.

Gravatt was in the dugout on crutches. Drunk and fighting in a 7-Eleven parking lot after the RATHCO games, Gary had fractured his metatarsal bones on some guy's ribs. He had intervened when the guy began to slap around his girl. They were both complete strangers to Gravatt.

"He was punching her around," Gary told me, leaning on his crutches. "I told him that shit didn't go around me. The fool started throwing at me. So I knocked him down and was kicking him in the ribs when the bitch jumps me and I break my foot. She was all over me clawing and scratching. Can you believe it?"

"You're asking the wrong person," I said.

35 ◇ July 1993

"HOW WE DO IN July will decide whether we qualify for the tournaments," I said.

"Thanks a lot, Dad," Carter said. "Thanks for coaching. Thanks for doing all the work you do so we can have a baseball team."

Win or lose, after nearly every game, Carter thanked me for doing what fathers are supposed to do; what my father had done.

"Hey, guys." Mike Wisser walked in, tall and lean. His brown hair splayed down across his forehead nearly covering both eyes. Then Carter and Wisser went up to Carter's room, sat in front of the air conditioner, and watched *Beavis and Butthead*.

The phone rang. It was Sonny Gold calling from Wimberley.

"What's going on down there, Sonny?" I asked.

"Most of the real estate people have gone bust, Gent," he said. "Your house is still for sale. Me and Laurel were talking; if your ex–old lady sells it ol' Carter gets some money, don't he?"

"Yeah, he gets twenty percent. Keep me posted if it sells."

"Why, Gent, you act like you don't trust her." Sonny laughed. "What's going on up there?"

"Baseball, Judge. We got a Connie Mack team."

"I coached Little League down here in Wimberley for forty-five years, Pete," the JP said. "I even had a couple boys go to the pros. How is ol' Carter doing?"

"Good, he's really grown since you saw him. He's six two now."

"Well, tell him that all his old Wimberley buddies ask me about him all the time. You coming to Texas anytime soon?" he asked.

"Don't know, Judge. How are Laurel and the boys?"

"Fine. Remember, you and Carter are always welcome to stay with us." Sonny then said good-bye and the connection was broken.

It was a strange feeling. Ten years ago Sonny and Laurel Gold and their kids, a couple of deputy sheriffs, and a few other people in Wimberley, San Marcos, and Austin helped to keep Carter and me alive, finally getting us the room to leave Texas.

Ten years ago. In some ways, it seemed like yesterday.

Beavis and Butthead was over. Mike Wisser and Carter walked into the living room.

"Carter," I said, "Sonny called."

"Sonny Gold? How's Laurel?" Carter asked.

"Fine. They want to know when we're coming back."

"I'd sorta like to go back to Wimberley," Carter said. "I sure loved that house we had. Remember my room?"

"Yeah, it was a great house."

"You should have seen the house we used to live in in Texas," said Carter, turning to Wisser. "It was on the side of this mountain. It was huge. It was great. I had my own bathroom and my bedroom had a regular bed and a sofa bed and a whole wall of closets. My window looked out into the backyard and up Old Baldy . . ."

Suddenly he stopped and looked at me. I shrugged. Each of us knew what the other was thinking.

"Sorry, bub," I said.

"Maybe some of us guys will drive down there." Carter's enthusiasm waned. He turned his mind back to baseball. As he walked Mike to his car, he acted like he had completely forgotten Wimberley. But he hadn't. He never would.

◇

"How do we beat the Maroons?" I asked Carter. After Mike Wisser left, Carter and I were checking through the equipment. The Maroons game was in three days.

"We always take a while to warm up," Carter said. There was confidence in his voice. "So use Wisser as the starting pitcher in the first game, instead of Nuke. That way, we'll be warmed up and ready to play by the second game. Let Wisniewski pitch the second game and we'll blow them away."

Why hadn't I thought of that? Carter had the ability to give credit to other people for their skills without a touch of envy. His judgment was unclouded by anger or jealousy. He could dislike a player personally and still give him full credit for his abilities as an athlete.

Carter was checking the catcher's mask when he looked at me. "Say, Dad," he asked, "do you think we will ever have enough money so that I could have a car of my own?"

The question caused me physical pain. We had struggled financially ever since Carter and I had moved up from Texas in 1985.

"I don't think we'll have enough for a while, Carter," I said. "I've got to finish the novel I'm working on and then hope it sells. I only get half the income from all but my last book. I've still got alimony and Chapter Eleven payments to make. Then I—"

"Never mind," Carter interrupted, trying to save me the embarrassment. "Never mind, Dad. I don't need a car. Grandma lets me drive hers. Don't worry about it."

The divorce and expensive court battles had limited Carter's horizons drastically, destroying many of the plans and dreams I had for both him and his sister.

Until the divorce began in Texas, money was never a problem and Carter lived in a big house with his own bathroom and bed-

room and an eight-acre yard. We had a generous cash flow plus
the annuities I had purchased for Carter to come due on his
eighteenth, twenty-first, and twenty-fifth birthdays. They would have
paid for clothes, college, travel, cars, and eventually his own house.

But instead, his mother's lawyers got his annuities for their
kids and Carter moved from his big house on the hill into the
small cramped room where I had grown up.

I put a quarter century of effort into getting out of Bangor
and creating a future for my children. All of it was wiped away
in a matter of months and Carter was starting out at square one
in exactly the same place I had begun a half century earlier.
Unfortunately, a half century earlier there were more opportunities everywhere, even in Bangor. Today Carter faced a desperate
uphill battle to get an education and build a career.

My parents had raised my brothers and me as part of the
burgeoning middle class with the ever-increasing opportunities
that the America of the fifties and sixties offered. I was raising
Carter as a member of the permanent underclass.

As each year of Carter's childhood passed and with it the opportunities for him that only money could buy, I would grind my
teeth and watch him miss his chance. We stayed mired in debt.
The guilt of not being able to get him the things he wanted was
difficult to bear. Carter handled the deprivations better than I did.

"Maybe someday though, huh, Dad?"

"Yeah, Carter, maybe someday."

"Don't worry, Dad. We'll beat the Maroons," Carter said.
"They will be tough to hit if they throw Gest or Dunham. Those
guys throw smoke. They won't hit Nuke too hard. But to win
we've got to hit their pitching."

I was listening to him, but my mind was on money, not
baseball.

"We'll win one game for sure," Carter said as he repacked
the catcher's equipment. He looked at me. "What's the matter,
Dad? Something wrong?"

"No," I lied. "I was just thinking about the Maroons."

36 ◊ The Maroons Again

SO FAR THIS SEASON, the Maroons had lost only four or five out of thirty-plus games they had played all over the state and in Indiana and Ohio. They had played powerful teams sponsored not only by Wendy's but also by Little Caesars pizza chain, teams with even bigger budgets and larger talent pools than the Maroons had.

The Maroons were still undefeated in our league. We just had to beat them.

Alex, Carter's dog, jumped up in his lap and started licking his face. "Alex, come on." Carter rolled the little tricolored dog over on his back and began scratching his stomach. When he stopped, the dog pawed at him to start again. "Aw right, Al," Carter said, righting the dog and scratching his hindquarters. Alex began squirming with pleasure, his mouth open, his tongue hanging out. He looked like he was smiling.

Slowly Carter's calico cat, Ritz, began sneaking along the bookcase toward the boy and his dog. When the cat jumped from the bookcase onto Carter's lap, Alex flipped his head and knocked the cat onto the floor with his nose.

With Alex a half step behind, Ritz took off for the back porch and refuge on top of the microwave oven. They raced through the kitchen, nearly knocking over Carter's grandmother.

"Oh! Carter!" she said. "I'm gonna roast your cat and dog for dinner."

"Yeah right, Grandma." Carter smiled.

Carter heard the cat and dog rocketing back through the kitchen. "Look out, Grandma. Here they come again!"

This time, the little shelty was in the lead, cutting his turn through the kitchen door a little too wide and skidding to a dead stop against the dining room bookcase.

Carter turned and looked down in time to see the cat slam

headfirst into the dog's ass. Carter's laugh sounded more like a screech. "Did you see that?" He started laughing again. "Ritz ran headfirst into Alex's butt." Then began his high, hard, throaty laugh. I started laughing at him. Hearing his laugh flooded me with a great sense of relief.

Later that night, Dave Martin, the Coldwater coach, called me to say that they had beaten and tied Kalamazoo Too. "I figured you would want to know," Dave said. "Although I still can't figure out this point system. Every time I ask, Hinga just tells me 'Don't worry, Coldwater will qualify.' "

"That doesn't sound too promising for us," I said. "He really doesn't want us in that tournament."

"Well," Martin said, "we're killing everybody in this Battle Creek league, and we'll qualify for the Kalamazoo district out of there. I just called to bring you up-to-date."

"We got the Maroons tomorrow," I said. "We still set to play in Coldwater next Sunday? There is no way my kids can make the drive to Coldwater and back to Bangor then all the way back to Gull Lake the next day."

"I'll make motel reservations here for you," Dave said. "This friend of mine manages a nice place on the edge of town and he'll give you some sort of group rate."

We needed a group rate. Nobody had much money. Carter's grandmother ended up paying for all the motel rooms and food plus gas and oil for the Coldwater trip.

◇

The day of the Maroons game dawned beautiful. My back had forced me out of bed and I had gone through two pots of coffee by the time the sun came up.

Around 4:30 P.M., driving alone to the ballpark, between the golden day lilies blooming tall in the ditches and the carpets of blue cornflowers and white Queen Anne's lace spread up the embankments, I thought about the coming game. Maybe Hinga and his staff couldn't outcoach Carter and his plan would work. What a grand thing to see and gloat about—Carter outcoaching the Maroons staff all by himself.

The rap music from our dugout blared all the way up to the parking lot. I got out of the car and began unloading the gear. They were doing it again, playing mind games with the Maroons.

Mike Wisser and Steve Leonard parked next to me and grabbed the equipment bags, heading down to the field and the nasty lyrics of Snoop Doggy Dogg and Dr. Dre.

Naked from the waist up, Mike Wisniewski, Chris Christian, and Carter, along with Decatur's Mike Fusco and Greg Grosvenor, were already on the field warming up. They really wanted to irritate the Maroons. Playing rap music and taking infield practice half naked would do it.

Carter was right. It took us one game to hit our stride against the Maroons.

Mike Wisser pitched the first game. Chris Christian caught. Mike Wisniewski played first. Eric Finch took second base. The boys from Decatur, Mike Fusco and Greg Grosvenor, had short and third, respectively. Ben Finch was in left. Steve Leonard was in right. Carter was playing center field.

The Maroons didn't hit Wisser hard. But add a couple of key errors and our inability to hit in the first game and we came away with a 5–0 loss in five innings.

In the second game, I put Shaun Eisner in right field.

Otherwise the lineup was the same with Christian leading off the batting order followed by Wisser, Wisniewski, Grosvenor, Carter, Ben Finch, Fusco, Eric Finch, and Eisner.

Wisniewski was pitching the second game against the Maroons and he was angry. The Maroons bench jockeys were running their mouths at him about the "Whiz" on the back of his uniform and he didn't like it.

Wisniewski held the Maroons to two runs while we scored eight.

For all intents and purposes the game was over in the second inning when Mike Wisser got his revenge for being the losing pitcher in the first game. He hit a grand slam home run over the left-field fence at around the 320 mark.

The boys added two more in the second and one each in the fourth and fifth. When Carter pulled down the high fly ball to center field for the third and final out, the Maroons dugout was so quiet you could hear the crickets chirping.

Bangor had hammered the Kalamazoo Maroons, 8–2, and the Maroons left in quiet huff. It was weird. So unlike their teams of the past. They just picked up their equipment and left without shaking hands or exchanging a word.

The Maroons loss to Bangor was their only loss in our league and only their sixth or seventh of the season.

They could beat teams from Chicago and Detroit. The idea of losing to dinky little Bangor was just too hard to bear. Carter had outcoached the Maroons staff. It was too delicious to savor except in tiny sips.

"Call up the *Gazette* and make sure they put our win over the Maroons in the box scores," Carter said. "You know the Maroons aren't gonna do it."

He was right. They didn't.

37 ◇ The Last Magic Summer

BEFORE OUR REGULAR SEASON finale against Kalamazoo Too, Bangor qualified for the AABC Connie Mack State District Tournament.

Kalamazoo Too also qualified, so there was nothing on the line for last doubleheader with KTOO except pride and the chance to play two more games. It was an opportunity to just play baseball. Games played for fun. No pressure. No fear. No anger. Just baseball.

The late July sun was still high in a bleached blue sky when the game started. Smelling grass and dust and sweat, I sat in the shade of the dugout and watched the kids. I finally let Carter pitch. He did fine. It was the best of days and I will never see it again.

"I'm exhausted," said Carter, sitting down beside me after the second inning. "Pitching is hard work. I don't remember it being this hard in Babe Ruth."

"Now you've got more muscles and you're feeling them tire," I said. "Plus all that drinking and those drugs."

"Really? I'm gonna have to stop drinking a quart of tequila a day? I suppose you're gonna say no crack now too." Carter played out the joke and then turned serious. "Who else is in from our league?"

"Our league was given only one seeding in the Kalamazoo district, plus the Maroons as host team and one seeding in Grand Rapids," I said.

"Dave Martin is bringing Coldwater out of the Battle Creek League," I continued. "I'm glad Dave did. Otherwise, Hinga might have been forced to refigure our win–loss and the point system." KTOO was 18–5–3 to our 19–6–1.

"So, how many teams from our league will be in the district?" Carter's eyes were bright. He was exhausted but excited about pitching.

"Just three in Kalamazoo," I repeated. "KTOO's coach agreed to go to the Grand Rapids district."

"Grand Rapids has got to be an easier district," Carter said.

"I asked KTOO's coach to take Grand Rapids as a favor," I said. "He knew we had difficulty getting enough kids to the games in Kalamazoo because of tight work schedules."

"That was nice of him." Carter began rubbing a new ball in his hands. "Just getting to Kalamazoo is a pain. Getting to Grand Rapids would have been impossible."

"Also, the only game being played at Western's stadium was the first game against the Grand Rapids Athletics," I said. "I knew you guys would want to play there."

"Absolutely." Carter stopped rubbing the ball. "Only one game at Western? Where are the rest of the games played?"

"Vicksburg, with that pissant short left-field fence for all the Maroons right-handed power hitters," I complained.

"The Maroons field?" Carter frowned. "Everybody was really looking forward to playing at Western."

"So was I." I patted his leg. "I loved it there."

Since meeting the Grand Rapids Athletics on the manicured grounds of Western Michigan University's baseball stadium would be the last time we would play there, we had to make it memorable. And, if we caught a break or two, we might achieve our second goal, making it to the championship game, where the Maroons would most likely be waiting.

Unless Dave Martin's Coldwater team finally played the game they were capable of and beat the Maroons in the first round. Coldwater was good and the Maroons had barely escaped losing to them in the regular season. Maybe in the tournaments . . . ?

It was what made a game a game.

We split the doubleheader with KTOO.

The regular season had ended.

38 ◇ Disaster in the Dugout

AS USUAL, AT ANNUAL tournament time disaster struck. It happened every summer, because the tournaments always coincided with long-planned family vacations and the blueberry harvest was going full-bore with dawn-to-dusk jobs suddenly available to high school kids who desperately needed the money.

Although I was always fully expecting to lose players at tournament time, replacing them was still a last-minute panic. There was no way to deal with the problem in advance. I had tried. My way of handling the problem was to wait with bemused interest to see the form the personnel disaster took and how the remaining kids responded to the setback. Their responses to adversity had never disappointed me.

This last summer's disaster was different only in numbers, names, and faces. I was not upset. I *was* surprised. The roster was literally gutted. The Finch twins quit to pick blueberries to save up money for Marine boot camp in San Diego. Brian Seymour left for vacation in Phoenix. The first day of the tourney Shaun Eisner couldn't get off work and Chris Christian had to work the day of the championship round. Greg Grosvenor and Steve Leonard both turned out to be a month too old to play in the tournaments.

After all the work, the planning, the hoping and praying, we had made it to the State District Tournament only to have the team fall apart within days of the first round. It was the most devastating loss of players I had experienced in all my summers. The tournaments were coming, and, if Bangor expected to last any length of time, we would have to completely rebuild our team.

Plus we needed more pitchers—several pitchers with lots of talent. Carter would have to find them.

"Are you mad at Ben and Eric for quitting and going to work?" Carter asked me.

"No, not really. That's who they are. I've coached them for years. Quitting is not unusual for them," I replied, then loosed a short laugh. "I'll tell you what is unusual: quitting to earn extra money for Marine boot camp."

We were on the couch, watching *Major League Baseball* on ESPN. Carter rested his head on my chest and I had my arm over his shoulder, allowing us to both stretch out. Alex the dog sprawled out on Carter's hip and rib cage.

"I'm kind of disappointed," Carter said. "I liked having them on the team. I can't believe they're going off to the Marines. I'm really gonna miss them."

"Well," I said, "right now, we've got to replace a lot of players. Who can we get?"

"Josh Lute from South Haven," Carter said. "He's good. He can pitch, hit, and play infield. We can use Josh Lute."

Carter began recalling and evaluating pitchers he had faced in the past high school and summer seasons. Kids he had known since grade school and junior high. Players he had watched for years. His memory was extensive and specific.

"Billy Coleman." Carter sat up suddenly. "Billy Coleman!"

Startled, the dog leapt to the floor.

"Billy brings gas and has the nastiest curveball and slider. Coleman can pitch and hit too. He'll play Division I."

"Have I seen him play?" I asked.

"During the high school season in Coloma." Carter nodded. "He hit that home run over the house beyond the left-field fence."

"He would be perfect." I remembered that baseball arcing out of the park like a Patriot missel. "What's he doing this summer?"

"Billy played Legion ball for St. Joseph," said Carter, leaning down and scratching Alex's chest. The dog jumped back in his lap. "Their season is over."

Carter cocked his head, began to rub his cheek with his long slender fingers, and frowned in thought. His brown eyes were blank for a while, then he turned to look at me. "You know, Wisniewski is always talking about his friend Mark from Chicago," Carter said. "He is a left-hander and Nuke swears the guy is great. If we could get Lute, Coleman, and Mark we would have a staff that could win the Tristate Regional."

The AABC Connie Mack district was double-elimination tourney. If we beat Grand Rapids and got the bye in the second round, we might need just one win in the championship round to take the title and proceed on to the Tristate Regional to face the top teams from Indiana and Ohio.

"I'll have to start trying to reach them tonight," I said. "It is only three days until the first game."

I called Coleman at home, introduced myself and explained our situation. He was polite and seemed pleased that we asked. After we cleared it with his mother, Billy agreed right away. I gave him the directions to Western's stadium.

"Well," I said to Carter who had been watching and listening the whole time, "Billy Coleman will play for us."

"Diggity!" Carter grabbed air with his right fist and pulled it back toward himself in a gesture of success. "Coleman has got mad skills! He is one of the best around. Wait'll you see him. He's got about five pitches, including three different curveballs. Billy is one mac daddy player." Carter's lips were relaxed in a smile, his brown eyes bright with excitement. "Start calling those other guys."

I followed his instructions and got players from nearby South Haven and far-off Chicago. It was hectic and slightly unnerving to call at eleven at night and cajole kids I didn't know to come and play for Bangor with only a couple days' notice. Billy Coleman, Josh Lute, and Wisniewski's buddy from Chicago Mark Gola, all agreed to join our team. I found another pitcher, Jace Canall, who had just finished his summer season, though he could play the first day only. We put these four new players on our tournament roster.

A couple weeks earlier, after the Finch twins quit, we added Chris Conley from Bangor, Mike Parker from Hartford, and Felix Reyna from Lawrence.

"Conley, Parker, and Reyna haven't played since the high school season ended in May. But they've had six games to get in shape," I said, poking Carter in the ribs. He had been cat-napping on the couch between phone calls.

"They've played with us for a couple weeks now." Carter yawned, stretched, and pushed me off the couch into the big white leather wing chair that his grandmother had had since the flood. "That'll be enough practice. Parker is hitting good already."

"At least Josh Lute and Billy Coleman have been playing all summer," I said. I leaned back in the chair. "Wisniewski says Mark's been pitching for a team out of Chicago. Canall is an unknown."

"We'll have seven new players for the Grand Rapids game," Carter said. "That's half our roster. Whether they've had any practice or not we need them. Don't worry."

Don't worry? Worrying seemed to be the biggest part of my job. The great qualities of Carter and his friends were their pride and confidence in each other. These kids were relentless, defining and redefining themselves to survive, inventing and reinventing themselves to prevail in the face of ignorance and future dread. Having suddenly lost eight of our players for all or part of the tournaments, which would have been a disaster to any other team, was treated as everyday stuff by Carter and his teammates.

When we had replaced the departed players, the team assimilated the new players as friends, teammates, and partners in the struggle. Quickly they reevaluated the situation as improving our chances in the tournaments. We could beat the Maroons in the district. We had beaten them before in the difficult five-inning format that played into the Maroons's strengths and against our weaknesses. So who knew what we might do against them in full seven-inning tournament games? A couple of breaks and anything was possible.

39 ◇ The Night Before

SITTING ON THE FRONT steps, watching the clouds turn purple-red as the sun set into Lake Michigan, I thought about tomorrow's first game against Grand Rapids at Western Michigan. It didn't seem possible so much time had passed.

In 1991, when Carter played in his first tournament at Western's stadium, he had just turned fifteen. That wonderful day on that radiant and glorious field, the end of Carter's Connie Mack summer baseball career had seemed light-years away. I thought Carter and I would have lots of time left together.

Now, suddenly, all that time was gone. I was rounding third and heading into home without a clue; I didn't know whether to stand, slide, shit, or go blind.

From now on, to keep the season going as long as possible,

we would have to keep winning games against teams that would just get better and better.

Time had run through my hands like water so fast, that my palms were already dry and beginning to crack. The future was now.

The screen door banged behind me and I recognized Carter's footsteps on the porch.

"What's up?" Carter stood next to me. "What've you been doing?"

"Worrying," I said. "What did you think?"

"That's what I thought. Don't worry. We're gonna be good, Dad," Carter said, and sat next to me. "We're a good team, really."

"What about ..." I began in my usual black way of looking at things.

"Lighten up, Dad." Carter put his forearm on my shoulder and leaned against me. "Coleman is a great pitcher. You still gonna pitch him against Grand Rapids?"

Carter and I had gone over the lineup several times the night before and I had decided to pitch Coleman first. I don't recall my reasons. But they were wrong. And all this time later, I can't think of one sensible reason why I used Coleman first in the pitching rotation.

If Coleman beat the Grand Rapids Athletics, that meant Mike Wisniewski would have to go against the winner of the Maroons-Coldwater game and both teams had faced Mike twice that summer. Grand Rapids had never seen Wisniewski, and, as far as I knew, the Maroons and Coldwater had never faced Coleman. Good coaching dictated the pitching order should be reversed; Nuke versus Grand Rapids and Coleman versus the Maroons or Coldwater. I *did not* reverse the order. Although Coleman and Wisniewski both pitched well and their performances had only positive effects on Bangor's games, my failure to make the right choice flouted the laws of probability.

"It's gonna be great to play there, isn't it?" Carter had

slipped his arm over my shoulder. "If I could play in a place like that," he said, "I would play baseball every day for the rest of my life. Imagine what it must be like in the major league parks."

There was a thought that twisted my head each time he mentioned it.

I recalled the games I had played for the Cowboys in Yankee Stadium, Forbes Field, Cleveland Municipal Stadium, Wrigley Field, and Busch Stadium in St. Louis. My first touchdown in Cleveland, my second at Forbes Field in Pittsburgh. Faded and dim, the memories were there. The god-awful mud in Cleveland in a cold December rain; my cleats suddenly hitting the sun-baked St. Louis infield dirt and nearly shattering my ankle during a hot September afternoon; the pastoral intimacy of Chicago's Wrigley Field and the ivy-covered brick wall that just angled lazily across the field and cut off the whole right corner of the end zone.

Finally, staring in senseless fright at the giant pictures of Ruth, Gehrig, and DiMaggio in the steel bowels of the old Yankee Stadium, shivering with fear at the incredible, terrible sense of history that filled every molding inch of the place. Because I had had to get my right leg shot up with Novocain and taped from hip to ankle, I had arrived early on that cold Sunday morning and couldn't shake the feeling I was lost in a crypt inhabited by the spirits of the damned of all sports. Death was there. The death that made sport so real.

I remembered all the stadiums. I couldn't remember me. Some other guy was living my life then. Mickey Mantle once told me, "Mickey Mantle was this other guy and I was just me living my life. It was very strange. I've never really understood it."

"Well," I finally answered Carter, through my distracting and disturbing recollections. "There are sure some beautiful parks. That place isn't bad."

"Are you nervous?" Carter asked.

"Yeah, my stomach is spinning."

"I got butterflies too," Carter said. "But, not the bad kind. The good kind, you know what I mean?"

"The good kind" was something no athlete ever forgot; the high-wire, razor-edged buzz of the adrenaline rush. We all got hooked and spent the rest of our lives trying to stay high or kick. And the greatest thing about youth was that the last rush was as good as the first, as long as you kept your mind and body healthy. It was the perfect drug. But eventually, of course, your body became an imperfect vehicle with injuries or the infirmities of age dulling the edge and stealing the high.

Mantle and I talked about the "rush" and the end one day in Dallas. Neither of us had played in over a decade. "Every day, I miss the excitement of the game and the guys, especially Billy [Martin] and Whitey [Ford]," Mickey said.

We were considering the prospect of Mantle turning fifty. He had never expected to live that long and had treated his body accordingly. By 1995, Mickey would need a liver transplant in a vain attempt to save his life.

"When I quit in '69 I never had any idea it would be this hard," Mantle continued. "I keep dreaming about making a comeback. Either I strike out or I hit a long ball into center and the fielder throws me out at first. When I wake up, I feel embarrassed and ashamed."

The game had invaded his dreams. Games do that.

Recently, I dreamed I was back at Michigan State playing for my old college basketball coach, a brilliant man with a temper as mercurial as Bobby Knight's. I was a three-time All–Big Ten player and hadn't seen the guy in over thirty years. Yet, I woke up scared and soaked in sweat. It was a terrifying dream.

"I dream I am in this taxi cab trying to get to Yankee Stadium," Mickey told me that long-ago day. "When I get there nobody will let me in. They don't recognize me.

"Finally, I find this hole in the fence and I am crawling through, when they announce the starting lineup," Mantle went on while I drank double vodkas. "The announcer is saying, 'Roger Maris . . . Yogi Berra . . . and number seven Mickey Mantle . . .' then I get stuck in the hole. That's when I wake up and I am sweating." I remembered the nervous energy that just radiated off his body as he put his thick forearms on the table and leaned toward me with his huge back and heavily muscled shoulders.

It was a melancholy day Mantle and I had spent together. Mickey had recently learned his boy Billy was desperately ill. "The only thing I really regret about baseball," Mickey said. "If I had to do it all again, I would be a better father."

Me too, Mickey. All of us would want to be better parents if we had to do it over. *That* was how life came packaged, with the toys on the top and the instructions and lessons learned buried deep beneath the broken hearts, broken marriages, banged-up bodies, cancers and scarred livers, to be discovered too late to avoid the irreparable damage.

The jump to Mantle's Yankee Stadium from that very place where Carter was going to play was so far as to be incalculable. Yet, only two short years previous, Carter played against Derek Jeter on that diamond and Jeter was making the long climb to play in Yankee Stadium.

The chance of a kid reaching the pro ranks was so infinitesimal that a player had to be crazy to think he had a chance. The great ones probably were crazy—a divine, and sometimes a real and deadly, madness that took them to the heights of fame and glory. To succeed as a professional athlete, a young man must throw caution and common sense to the winds. His success depends on a neurotic commitment, a psychotic-compulsive discipline, and a narcissistic, stone-blind belief in his own worth.

Crazy men. I know. I was one. I have the records, and the physical and mental scars to prove it. I actually believed I could play in the NBA. I was drafted by the old Baltimore Bullets and still believed I would have been an all-pro in the NBA if they had offered me more than $8,500 a season.

But when the NBA money didn't match the Dallas Cowboys's $11,000 offer, I immediately believed I could play in the NFL. Having not played football since high school, I was crazy enough to fly to the Cowboys' California training camp and join what would become the premier franchise in the NFL. I was on America's team's roster. The A list of America's guests. Crazy men.

Watching Carter on the steps, I wondered how far he was from the major leagues, how badly he wanted to get there and what I would do about it. Would I help him get there? Would I discourage him? In a sane world, professional sports was delusional. Yet, that night on our porch through the looking glass of sport, the life seemed valuable and quite harmless. Should I help him? Could I?

Carter playing professionally was not unreasonable. I had played. He had the physical skills and a lot more of the necessary character than I had had—80 percent of sports is above the neck. And despite everything, he had kept his head, his heart, his word, and his soul. He was becoming a man with the strong, honest personality traits that I wished I had had when I was his age, and now he was nearly grown and almost gone.

◇

Several weeks earlier, Carter had called me in to watch a television show about a Florida nursing home that sponsored a Little League team.

Old people with walkers and wheelchairs were yelling reedy encouragement to children so young that the show would have been absurd were it not so pure and beautiful a thing. A game was bridging generations of difference and disillusion to bring these people together for this incredible human communion . . . and that game was baseball.

I was beginning to know how the old folks felt. I had long been obsolete and was quickly becoming implausible, trying to cling to the rush vicariously through these kids. The spike was still stuck deep in my soul. Watching Carter and his friends play ball was my methadone program. From the years of sitting in dugouts I had reached a kind of truce with the absurdity and the hopelessness of life and, through these kids, I searched for peace of mind.

I would have to finish the search alone. But they had gotten me up and on the trail. As long as I kept moving forward, there was a chance for me to finish out my life without the last taste in my mouth being cold steel and gun oil.

◇

As I watched Carter, I remembered something else Mickey Mantle had told me. It was about his first one-hundred-thousand-dollar contract.

"I'd had a great year but there was still some hard feelings about it." He smiled that charming country boy smile. "What nobody every wrote about was the next season I didn't do as well and they cut my salary. Hell, I loved the game. I woulda played for free."

Years ago, most of the guys I knew with the Cowboys felt exactly the same way. At least, for a while.

Watching Carter and thinking of Mickey, it became clear to me—life wasn't all that absurd and hopeless after all. No matter how badly my generation messed up, Carter's generation still carried the future with it and had the character and humanity necessary to redeem us all.

Carter may or may not live out his sports dreams—that is between him and him. But the thing he would never do was give up on the dream he finally did choose. Carter would find his way. He would reach his goals. He would become *the player* in the grandest sense of all—he would become a *good man*.

40 ◇ The AABC Connie Mack State Tournament—Day One

WE ARRIVED TO FACE the Grand Rapids Athletics at Western Michigan's baseball stadium at noon to allow the team lots of batting practice and time to get themselves mentally ready. Game time was one-thirty.

The temperature was in the high seventies under a bright blue sky. The sunlight was strained and softened by high, stringy, cirrus clouds. The green painted grandstands seat neatly into the ridgeline, blended with the leafy oak and maple trees covering the bank of the natural bowl. Below, the baseball field lay in all its grass-green, white-lined, God-blessed splendor.

Convinced they could win the tournament, the old players and the new players began talking, throwing balls around, and jogging to work up their legs. Watching them warm to one another in the new uniforms with their names on the back, I realized that this was the first time we had played in an AABC Connie Mack State District and not violated the matching uniform rule. We had come a long way in three years.

The boys looked good in gray with the red cursive "Bangor" lettering and block numbers on the front and back. I was proud of the sight of Carter in his uniform against the green of the field. Young men and baseball on a perfect day in a fine park. I was just loving the whole spectacle. I would have gladly stayed in that moment forever—when anything and everything was still possible.

In the batting cage, Carter began to hit the ball steadily. His stroke seemed right, he was meeting the ball sharp and hard, and there was a good snap in his wrists. Though still lacking heavy muscles, Carter worked constantly on form and fundamentals for power in his hitting.

Since life had fallen apart in Texas years ago, this was what I had wanted for Carter all those long summers: one more splendid day in the sun, one more game played on this glamorous ground to show him what he was truly capable of in the real world. One more day of ecstatic experiences that would help him to cope with the pain and sorrows that haunted his past and waited in his future.

Carter and his teammates had a long, tough road to ride into the twenty-first century and my generation had done little to help. Were discipline, dedication, commitment, teamwork, and respect for the game and each other the principles that would keep them on course? I hoped so.

The Grand Rapids Athletics had filled the third base dugout and were beginning to warm up.

Slowly, the Bangor players began to trickle back from the batting cages and the field.

The umpires arrived.

Looking harassed and hurried by his job as tournament director, Mike Hinga dropped into our dugout and asked for my roster. As he called off the names, I handed him the birth certificates. He left quickly for the other first-round game between the Maroons and Coldwater being played at the same time thirty miles south in Vicksburg.

After Mike left, I watched the Athletics take infield practice.

They knew the game. Big kids, confident, picked from the Class A and B schools around Grand Rapids, they moved about the field with the easy grace of seasoned young men.

The umpires signaled for the Grand Rapids coach and me to come to the plate and discuss the ground rules. The Athletics coach was one of those old baseball guys like Dave Martin from Coldwater. I knew both umpires from previous games in Connie Mack. They were good at their jobs and enjoyable to be around.

I won the toss and Bangor was home team. Everything was all right, so far. The game would be seven innings unless one team had an eight-run lead after five innings of play. The mercy rule.

Billy Coleman took the mound and Chris Christian was catching. Wisser was at first, warming up Mike Parker at second; Wisniewski was at third with Fusco at short stop.

In the huge outfield, Carter looked lonely in center, flanked by Josh Lute in left and Felix Reyna in right. The size of the outfield was frightening. I remembered how two years back only the blazing speed of Derek Payne, the right fielder we picked up from River Valley, had saved us in the extra-innings win over Coldwater.

We were aiming higher than third this year. We were going after the Maroons, the championship, and a seed in the Tristate Regional. The regional that had often delivered the national champions.

But first we had to get past the Athletics and they didn't look like they were going to give up easy. Their first batter had a full count before he hit a hard single into left center. Coleman was a careful, deliberate pitcher. The second batter hit a fly to center that Carter took coming forward on the run, so he could quickly make the throw to Parker the cutoff man and hold the runner on first. A single to right center moved the first base runner to third and Grand Rapids had men on the corners with one out. These kids hit the ball hard.

Billy bore down on the next two batters, getting one to hit a fast grounder to Wisniewski, who held the runner on third then rocketed the ball to first in time to catch the hitter. The final batter went down swinging and we were out of the top of the first, unscathed. But the power of the Grand Rapids hitters was obvious. They were capable of breaking the game open at any time. It was a worrisome thought.

Leading off for Bangor, Chris Christian hit the ball straight back to the pitcher, then got all the way to second on a throwing error. He moved to third on Mike Wisser's single. When the Grand Rapids catcher made the throw but failed to catch Wisser stealing second, Chris beat the throw back to the plate and scored our first run. Then Mike Fusco struck out. Mike Wisniewski and Billy Coleman both went down on infield flies. We led at the end of the first, 1–0.

Top of the second, Coleman struck out the first batter and gave up a single to the second man up. The base runner stole second. Fusco made a great play on a ball hit in the hole behind second, getting the hitter at first but allowing the man at second to reach third. Then Billy got his second strikeout of the inning, stranding the runner ninety feet from home.

There was no doubt: Billy was the real thing. Yet, Grand Rapids hit him hard enough to start me smoking by the top of the third inning. Smoking kept me from giving useless advice.

Parker began our half of the inning with a walk. Carter got a full count, then struck out. Lute and Reyna walked to fill the bases. The Grand Rapids pitcher couldn't find the plate. Finally, he began throwing strikes at Christian, and Chris drove a single into right center, scoring Parker and Lute.

With Wisser at bat, Reyna got tagged out at third as he and Christian attempted a double steal. Wisser hit into left center for a single and Christian scored from second. Fusco ended the inning grounding out to the shortstop. We were leading, 4–0, going into the first half of the third.

Facing the top of their order again, Coleman gave up a single. The second batter drove a grounder to Parker at second and he tossed it over to Fusco for the front end of a double play, but Fusco made a bad throw to first. The runner continued on to second base. Fusco redeemed himself by fielding a tough grounder, holding the runner on second and then making the play at first.

We had two down and a man on second when the Grand Rapids' cleanup hitter took Coleman's fastball for a double into deep left center, scoring the man on second. Unfazed, Billy came right back and struck out the next batter on three straight pitches.

The bottom of the third began as Wisniewski grounded out to the pitcher. Coleman reached first on an error by the shortstop. Parker was hit by a pitch. Carter was up with Coleman on first and Parker on second. He was down 0–2, then snapped a single to right, scoring Parker.

Josh Lute followed with another single, scoring Coleman. Lute was thrown out trying to steal second and Reyna grounded out to second. We went into the top of the fourth inning leading, 6–1.

It was three up and three down for the Athletics in the top of the fourth. Things looked pretty good. But these Grand Rapids kids were good. A five-run lead could disappear pretty fast if they ever got to Coleman.

Chris Christian led off our half of the fourth with a single and Mike Wisser did the same. Fusco popped out to third. Then, Billy Coleman stepped into the box, set himself in his peculiar canted stance, and drilled the first pitch like a rocket to deep right center field. Seeing the fly ball was uncatchable, Christian and Wisser took off. Steve Leonard, coaching at third base, waved them home. Coleman went into third for a stand-up triple.

After holding their collective breath for four innings, everybody went crazy. Grand Rapids was a damn good team and we were beating them, 8–2, in the bottom of the fourth.

I reminded the players that we were playing seven innings and there was plenty of time left for Grand Rapids to rally. Then, I sat back in the dugout and tried to stay out of the way as Parker popped out to third to end the inning.

I couldn't relax. Bangor had to hold the lead for three more innings. It seemed probable. But the power of the Grand Rapids hitters continued to keep me unnerved and lighting cigarettes.

The Athletics started off the top of the fifth with a single and Grand Rapids players began to pick up their dugout chatter, their spirits buoyed. Skilled, confident players, they were ready for the certain rally that would lead them to a victory over this little town team.

Coleman struck out the next batter, picked off the guy on first, and the Grand Rapids dugout quieted. Suddenly, they had nobody on and two outs. It took a little of the steam out of them. Then Billy walked the next two batters and Grand Rapids came right back to life, sensing a rally again. Their bench was on their feet as their catcher walked to the plate.

In the third, this guy had hit the long double to left center. Coleman went right at him and blew two strikes by his knees. But the Grand Rapids batter was ready on the third pitch and Billy had let the ball get up a little too high.

The big catcher swung from his heels, nailing a hard drive to deep center field. Carter froze for an instant, gauging the trajectory of the ball, then turned and ran for the fence.

Reyna was already on the dead run from right.

The guy had hammered the ball with two men on base. I could see our comfortable lead slipping away and a monster rally taking us right out of the game. My heart stopped.

The world stopped.

For a moment, the only people in that park who were moving were the batter, the base runners, and Carter and Reyna who were both driving for deep right center racing the ball to the fence.

I felt dizzy and sick, holding my breath, watching the arc of the ball and the long desperate strides of Carter's lean legs. Felix had started out too far away. Carter was the only one with a chance at the ball, if it even stayed in the park.

Carter looked back once to pick up the ball's flight in the air, then turned, doing the geometry in his head as he ran. Reyna changed his angle and headed toward the infield because the ball was going so deep we needed two cutoff men to get it to home. Mike Parker dashed into the deep infield as the second cut-off man. Coleman came off the mound to back up Wisniewski at third. Wisser went home to back up Christian.

The first base runner was crossing the plate, the second runner was nearly to third, and the hitter was heading to second, supremely confident. He *had* hit a rope.

Everything suddenly went into slow motion, as Carter took one long, last, desperate stride, looked up and reached out with his glove to pull in the ball for the third out.

Reyna pulled up smiling and waited for Carter. The two jogged toward the dugout together. Carter was shaking his head the whole way. Coleman strolled across the infield as calm as a man out walking his dog.

Finally, I exhaled and my head started spinning. I was nauseous. Then my heart started again.

Pumped up by their near-death experience, the players came off the field more confident than ever. Carter followed up his catch by leading off the bottom of the fifth, striking out on three straight pitches. He came back to the dugout totally disgusted with himself.

"I'm not seeing the ball," he told Mike Wisser.

Mike immediately began a long treatise on the problems with Carter's stance, because that was what Mike always did when anybody had a problem. If you didn't want Wisser's advice, you didn't talk about your problems.

Josh Lute took a base on balls.

Felix Reyna walked up to the plate and took the first pitch for a called strike. Felix hit the second pitch on a line over the right fielder's head all the way to the fence for another triple, scoring Lute.

Now, it was bedlam on our side of the field. All the pent-up anxieties and expectations of the whole summer seemed to be pouring out of these players in an exuberant display and celebration of their skills. Every miserable ache and pain and worry of the summer was worth it to me at that moment. That moment that could never be taken away and would never come again.

I sat back in the corner of the dugout and watched the boys congratulate each other. Their faces beamed like vapor lights in the fog. They couldn't stop smiling, laughing, and hugging. They had come to play and had done it well. The air hummed with their energy. The sky seemed bluer. The day was suddenly more radiant and real. Things had happened here. Important things that some would remember forever.

They were going to win. They knew it now.

Grand Rapids was damn good and on another day they might have won. But not on this day. This game was in the win column and it was only the fifth inning.

The game ended suddenly in the bottom of the fifth. With Reyna tripled to third, Christian walked and stole second. Wisser nailed a hard single into center and Christian and Reyna both scored. The game was over, 11–2. The mercy rule: an eight-run lead after five innings.

Now we had to drive immediately to Vicksburg to play the winner of the Coldwater-Maroons game. And, despite all wishing to the contrary, we all knew who that would be.

41 ◇ The Tournaments—Game Two

"DAD?" CARTER SPOKE UP. We were driving from Kalamazoo to Vicksburg. Felix Reyna was riding with us. "What about Jace Canall? You asked him to come all the way here to play."

"I know," I said. "I was planning to put him in to pitch the sixth and seventh inning against Grand Rapids." Which was true. Canall was warming up when Wisser knocked in the winning runs and ended the game.

"He can only play today," Carter said. "You better play him."

"For who?" I asked. "He told me he is a pitcher but does play some infield. I've never seen him play."

"You can put him in for me," Carter said, getting me off the hook, as he had so many times before. And, like an idiot, I agreed. Again, I let Carter pay for being the coach's son. It would prove to be the costliest mistake of the day.

The Maroons won the coin toss and were the home team.

With the exception of my replacement of Carter with Canall, the same guys played the Maroons game, although the pitching change required moving positions; Wisniewski was pitching. Mike Parker moved out to left field to make room for Billy Coleman at second base and Josh Lute took over at third for Wisniewski.

The top of the first, the Maroons pitcher retired Christian, Wisser, and Fusco on three straight strikeouts. There was no doubt. The Maroons were coming after us. They wanted to show there was no way we were going to beat them again this season.

Not in the tournament. No quarter would be given. And I played right into their hands.

But we could beat them. We had the talent. What we didn't have was the coaching. The Bangor players would just have to take up the slack like they had done for years.

Wisniewski faced four batters in the bottom of the first, giving up one hit and no runs.

The score was 0–0, when Wisniewski grounded out to the pitcher to open the second inning. Billy Coleman waited out a base on balls and immediately stole second. Parker grounded out to short and Jace Canall struck out to end our half of the inning. By the top of the third, the score was still 0–0. We could not score in our half of the inning.

In the bottom of the third Mike Fusco booted a grounder and the first hitter reached first. The Maroons were now back to the top of their order. Wisniewski struck out their leadoff hitter. But their number two man hit for a double and the runner scored. Mike put down the next two batters and the third inning ended. We were down, 0–1, going into the fourth.

Errors had killed us all summer long and here we were up against the Maroons with five new players on the field. And I still had Carter on the bench.

Carter had worked hard for years, earning this day, and I had let him take the fall for me. This wasn't some intricate baseball maneuver that had eluded me to the kids' expense. This was just bad manners and stupidity. All was lost by that decision.

It was still 0–1 Maroons in the bottom of the fourth. They had two outs with a man on second when the batter hit a routine fly ball to center. It should have been the third out. But, I still had Carter on the bench. Canall, in Carter's spot, misjudged his angles and the ball bounced off his glove. The runner scored from second.

Wisniewski got the third out on strikes. Mike was angry. He was pitching a good game and we were losing, 0–2. Errors were killing us. And, except for Fusco, they all came from kids having to play in positions to which they weren't accustomed.

So what did I do? I put Carter in for Reyna.

When Bangor went back out into the field, Carter would return to his spot back in center. Canall would move to right and still be playing out of position. And, to add injury to insult, Reyna had tripled against Grand Rapids just two hours earlier.

I wanted to cry. I smoked a cigarette with the filter torn off instead. It was a way of punishing myself.

The bottom of the fifth was a nightmare. Mike Fusco made his second error of the game to put the leadoff man on first. The second batter flew out to Carter in center.

Fusco, who hadn't had four errors all season and routinely made spectacular plays at shortstop, had back-to-back errors for his third and fourth of the game.

Wisniewski calmed himself and studied the loaded bases. The Maroons had one out, and, despite everything, they hadn't scored. Mike got the next batter to pop up to him. Now the Maroons had two outs and the bases loaded.

The next batter hit what looked to be an easy fly ball to right which would end the inning and we would get out unscathed. But, I had moved Canall to right when I replaced Reyna with Carter. Again, he misjudged the ball, letting it get past him. When he finally got to it, he threw a perfect strike to the plate and that kept the third man from scoring. Apparently he could pitch but catching he couldn't handle.

Wisniewski walked to the mound from backing up the plate and looked over at me. I knew what he was thinking. And he knew I knew. I shrugged my shoulders. The damage was done. I could not unmake my mistakes.

Not surprisingly, Wisniewski finally gave up a hit and the third run of the inning scored. Coleman threw out the next batter from second and the fifth was over. After a flurry of errors we trailed, 0–5.

Wisniewski threw his glove in the corner of the dugout.

"This is nobody's fault but mine," I said, saying it before somebody beat me to it. Hell, it had worked for Robert E. Lee at Gettysburg. "It is all my fault. I made bad decisions."

I had lost the game before it began, in the car on the drive to Vicksburg. Mental errors had killed Bangor that day, and I made them.

The game ended, 0–5. Again, the Maroons left the field as if we weren't even there. They were good, but not that good. Given half a chance, Bangor could beat those guys. Today, I had taken away more than half of Bangor's chance. Tomorrow would be different—depending on how the coin toss went.

42 ◇ The Edge

THE CALL FROM MIKE HINGA came at 11:30 P.M. that night. "Make sure you have Billy Coleman down in your regular season score book as having played at least three games," he said.

"Okay." My voice betrayed no reaction. Hinga was up to something. I wasn't going to ask. He mentioned only Coleman. Why hadn't he mentioned the six other guys I had picked up? What did he mean put Coleman in my score book? Coleman was the right age. He was on my tournament roster. The only roster I ever turned in all year.

"By the way," Hinga added. "You won the toss. Bangor got the bye into the championship round."

"The kids will be happy," I replied calmly. After three years, Bangor had finally reached the championship round.

"How will the pairings work?" I asked.

"If Grand Rapids beats us in the first game tomorrow," Hinga replied, "then we will have to play Grand Rapids again to see who qualifies to play Bangor for the championship. You won't play again until the following day."

Hinga seemed to be gritting his teeth.

"So?" I talked slowly. "You might have to play Grand Rapids twice tomorrow and we wouldn't play until the next day?"

"Yeah," Hinga said, "that's a possibility. But if we win, then we play you in the second game tomorrow for the State District Championship."

"That sounds good," I replied. Hell, it sounded great. If Grand Rapids could beat the Maroons tomorrow, we would have to win only one more game to advance to the Tristate Regional.

"Remember," Hinga repeated, "Coleman has to be in your regular score book for three games."

I didn't reply. One thing I had learned in three years of trying to deal with Hinga—if he asks for the time, don't tell him how to make a watch. What was the problem with Coleman and why did it involve only Billy? We had picked up players every year for the tournaments.

For the first time ever, we were in the championship round of the AABC Connie Mack State District Tournament with a possibility of winning and moving into the Tristate Regional. Finally, the championship was within our grasp.

I called into the front room where Carter, Mike Wisser, and Chris Christian were drinking pop and eating the soft tacos Carter's grandmother was making for them.

"Yeah," said Carter, leaning over his napkin, as lettuce and salsa dropped from between the folds of his flour tortilla. "What's going on?"

"We're in the championship round. We won the toss. Grand Rapids and the Maroons play tomorrow first game. If Grand Rapids beats the Maroons, they have to play again. We have to beat the winner to take the State District Championship."

There it was. We were possibly within one win of the State District title and a seed in the Tristate Regional. The thought was just too delightful to think about. It gave me butterflies. The boys were excited.

Their celebration was subdued by the day's 0–5 loss and the fact that tomorrow Chris had to work at the video store and would be unavailable to catch. So Wisser or Wisniewski would have to catch, and, either way, it took a top pitcher out of our rotation for the most important game we would ever play.

Carter and Wisser called and explained to their teammates

the various ramifications of being in the championship round. Bangor had qualified as one of the top Connie Mack teams in southwest Michigan. With luck, in a couple of days we would be the top team.

If we won the District, we would be matched up against the top teams from Indiana, Ohio, and Michigan. Talented, big-money teams sponsored by Wendy's, Little Caesars, Time-Warner, and Disney. The Tristate Regional was serious business.

Only two years after Carter and the others had risked death and dismemberment by Shane Sheldon during our first AABC Connie Mack State Districts, Bangor had made it to the championship round—two wins, at most, away from the Tristate Regional.

Carter and his teammates were amazing . . . and they were almost gone—there wouldn't be athletes with talent and attitude like this in Bangor again for a long time . . . if ever again.

But I couldn't think about that. I had to think about tomorrow and how to patch up the big hole left by the loss of our catcher, while at the same time praying for Grand Rapids to do our dirty work and beat the Maroons. The Athletics were capable of beating them, at least once. That's all we needed them to do, beat the Maroons once. Surely they could do that. Surely.

43 ◇ The Championship Round

AT VICKSBURG THAT NEXT DAY, Grand Rapids looked like the powerhouse team I thought they were when we had faced them the day before. The Athletics seemed to be in control of the game, holding a lead and hitting the ball well. Kalamazoo's fans were obviously dismayed, as the Grand Rapids fans took heart at the Athletics's lead.

The game was a slugfest. The teams went at each other like sumo wrestlers. It was a display of serious baseball talent. The

Maroons battled desperately from behind and were losing going into their half of the final inning. If Grand Rapids could hold out in the seventh, then the Athletics and the Maroons would have to play again, with the survivor playing Bangor the next day for the State District title.

And, on that day, we would have Chris Christian, our catcher, back, plus a rested and complete four-pitcher rotation ready to throw a mere seven innings.

All Grand Rapids had to do now was hang on.

Unfortunately, the Maroons were true to form, a seventh-inning rally tied the game and sent it to extra innings. They were good. You had to give them that. They came through. The Maroons played when needed and won games when they had to win them.

Grand Rapids was a talented team and they were giving as good as they got. They seemed to be a match for Kalamazoo. Yet, I had no doubt we would beat Grand Rapids. We had beaten them once and now they were wearing themselves out battling the Maroons. They would be drained by their victory. We would beat Grand Rapids.

But Grand Rapids blew their chance to beat the Maroons, failing to finish them off in the seventh. I had played them enough times to know that—never ever let the Maroons back up.

Now the Maroons were unbeatable. Grand Rapids was doomed.

Bangor would have to beat the Maroons two games in a row. It had taken us two complete Connie Mack seasons and three tournaments to win two games from the Maroons. Now, we would have to beat them twice, back to back.

These were not good odds. We had the talent to beat them. It was all a question of execution, all in the head. Mental mistakes would destroy us.

We *had* to win. The alternative was too depressing to be considered.

This terrible battle the Maroons were waging against the Athletics would not wear the Maroons down, or cost them that fine edge they always had. They could field two teams of almost equal ability. If Grand Rapids was in a struggle with one Maroons team, the other Maroons team was sitting in the shade of their dugout resting and waiting for us.

The Maroons bullpen was eight or ten pitchers deep, the quality dropping only slightly when you got to their fifth or six pitcher. They actually had brought in "closers" against us before, in the five-inning games.

Feeling the July sun beat through my shirt, I stood next to the crowded bleachers, watching and considering our prospects. Today might be the last day I coached Carter in summer baseball. Never again would I be so deeply involved with him in a sport.

It was nearly over. I still didn't really understand what "it" was, I just knew I didn't want it to end and the only way to continue was by winning baseball games. I would do anything to keep winning. In just a couple of hours, those summers that I thought would last forever would simply cease. No more long days in the sun with Carter and his friends. No car rides to away games with excited, laughing kids. No more being an intregal part of their summer, a confidant treated as an equal, a friend, a companion, and teammate. No more being caught up in the excitement of a well-played game. No more hours spent celebrating and replaying the victories. No more commiserating over a loss, then rising above defeat to go on to win the next game.

There would be no next game.

Endings were not new to me. One day ten years earlier my ex-wife sent two armed men to tell me my marriage was over. One day we were a family. The next day we were not a family. I had suffered the endings of high school, college, and professional careers in sports. They had all been painful, confusing experiences that cut the ground from beneath my self-esteem and identity. One day I was a player and the next day I was not a player; the difference was profoundly dreadful and bewildering.

But this was something else entirely.

Summer baseball had bound us so tightly for so long, it hadn't dawned on me that my life would forever be affected if we lost today.

I shivered involuntarily at the realization and my whole body was coated with a thin, cold sweat. I watched the Maroons and Grand Rapids still tied in extra innings.

Looking at Carter, his jersey unbuttoned revealing his tanned, bony chest and hard, flat stomach, I wondered what was next for us. We had already been through so much. We had been bound together for so long, it was impossible to imagine Carter breaking away. But he would. And it could start today.

Carter was talking with Mike Wisser. He smiled and burst into his incredible laugh, I bathed in the sight and sound. Finally, reluctantly, knowing full well Grand Rapids would lose, I pulled out my roster and walked to the car, wondering if I could find two ways to beat the Maroons.

First, I had to select a pitcher. My first choice, Mike Wisser, had to catch in place of Chris Christian.

Mike Wisniewski's arm was sore after throwing seven innings in vain yesterday. Nuke said he would pitch if I wanted him. But I had enough guilt, I did not want the responsibility of blowing out a seventeen-year-old kid's arm.

Billy Coleman was noncommital and I figured I'd use him in relief or as a closer. I had never seen Josh Lute pitch and no-body told me until too late that he was an excellent pitcher.

Wisser would catch and Mark Gola would pitch. Wisniewski moved to first to replace Wisser, Coleman was at second, Fusco at short, and Lute at third. Carter was back in center with Felix Reyna in right and Mike Parker in left.

Shaun Eisner had gotten off work, so I had one extra player.

Wisser warmed Mark up and came to me in the dugout with glowing reports. "His fastball is incredible," Wisser said. "It's a lot like Nuke's with more movement."

"Does he have a curve?" I asked. "A knuckleball, slider, any-thing else?"

"I don't need anything else," Mark said. "I'll take these guys out with my fastball.'' Yesterday he had watched Grand Rapids and the Maroons from the dugout. He was not impressed by either team and made no bones about it. His open confidence made me ambivalent. Maybe he was as overpowering as he thought. But the Maroons were not a third-rate club. What if he couldn't take them out with his fastball? Did he have other pitches? And, could he withstand the awful pressure of standing alone on the mound?

I would know soon. We won the toss and were the home team.

Warming up with Wisser behind the plate, Mark was throwing BBs at the knees. It appeared that he had the tools.

Donny Yant, the Maroons excellent and irritating third baseman, led off. Yant was a top player offensively and defensively. Most likely, he would continue to play at the college level. He seemed skilled enough to me.

How Mark fared with Yant would tell a lot.

Quickly, Mark had Yant down with two strikes. On the third pitch, Yant started to let the ball go. Then, at the last possible moment, Yant must have thought it was a strike. The Maroons third baseman took a little half swing at the ball, flaring a Texas Leaguer for a single. Goddamn aluminum bats!

After that, Mark threw eight straight balls.

As the Maroons number three batter walked to first to load the bases, I called time-out and went to the mound to talk to Mark and ask Wisser for advice. Mark seemed puzzled and a little edgy. He kept looking at his shoes. Mike and I tried to calm him down.

"He's not missing by much," Mike told me. "Some of them were perfect strikes—this umpire is screwing him over. I don't trust these umpires whenever we play the Maroons." He didn't trust the umpires. I wanted them on a polygraph after every pitch.

"Just put the ball in my glove," said Mike, turning to Mark with determination and confidence. "You just got to dig down and work your way out of this hole. You can do it."

After I walked back to the dugout, I lit a cigarette and started praying. If this was the *Titanic,* I had better start rearranging the deck chairs.

Mark's next four pitches were called balls. The hitter never took the bat off his shoulder. The pitches weren't that bad. Did the batter knew something I didn't? Then again, why prepare to swing when the pitcher has thrown twelve straight balls?

When I turned in my lineup card, nobody had questioned Mark's eligibility to play. At least, they hadn't said anything to me. Maybe something was said to the plate umpire? Because Mark's strike zone got smaller and smaller until it vanished completely.

I decided to throw Mark Gola from Chicago at the Maroons that day for two reasons. First, Nuke had said the southpaw Gola was his equal. Another Mike Wisniewski would be a rare find and a spectacular addition to the pitching rotation. Second, after Hinga's ominous call last night about Coleman I had decided to go ahead and get a ringer up on the mound right away that nobody in the area knew about and see what happened.

What happened was a disappearing strike zone. I should have seen it coming. I did see it coming—way back in May. Bangor wasn't going to be allowed to go too far—it was the only way the season could possibly end.

The Maroons' first run crossed the plate, forced in by the walk.

The bases were loaded and there were no outs. Mark was not getting any close calls and some of the close calls were right down the middle. He was just a kid and frustration quickly took his head away and that was it. Eventually, he walked a total of five batters in a row, throwing only three more strikes in the process. He threw a total of five strikes to six batters.

Calling time after the Maroons number six batter had walked and the third run had crossed the plate, I signaled for Billy Coleman and asked Mark where he felt comfortable on the field.

"I don't want to play anymore," he said. "I want to go home."

"Home?" I stuttered. "I . . . I can't take you home right now. Play a spot in the field . . ."

"No." Mark was determined. "I don't want to play anymore."

I sent Shaun Eisner into left field and Mike Parker over to second base to replace Billy Coleman.

"You weren't throwing that bad, Mark," I said back in the dugout. It was the truth. He had great speed. It was possible the umpire was missing the calls.

"Well, I haven't pitched in two years," he said, and turned away to sit down in the dugout.

What? I must have heard that wrong.

Walking to the corner of the dugout, I lit a cigarette, instead of falling away in a dead faint. "I haven't pitched in two years." Is that what he just said?

Why hadn't he mentioned that yesterday when he was impugning the Maroons and Grand Rapids. I had just started a pitcher in the most important game we had ever played and the kid hadn't stepped on the mound in two years. It was amazing he kept the ball in the park.

Coleman faced four batters, striking out two, walking one, and getting the third to fly out to Shaun Eisner in left.

We came to bat in the bottom of the first, down 0–4. It was not hopeless by any means. These kids were capable of coming back. Of course, so were the Maroons. They had just shown that against Grand Rapids. If pitcher Scott Wetherbee had trouble, Hinga had his number one pitcher Pat Dunham waiting for us in right field.

As Carter had said about Dunham so many times before, he brought "major gas."

Sachs, the Indiana scholarship player from Western Michigan University, was at second base. Yoshi Martin, who would become Sachs's teammate at Western, was in center field and Brad Block, who would be drafted out of high school along with Dennis Gest and Dunham, was in left. (By the summer of 1995, Dunham, Gest, and Block would be up in Alaska playing in the Cape Cod Wooden Bat League.)

Carter led off and singled to left to open our half of the first. Mike Wisser was up next. I could see he and Carter were exchanging signals. At the pitch, Carter made a break for second. They had put on the hit and run.

Carter got a good jump, but Wendt the catcher had called for a pitchout. Wisser tried to protect Carter by swinging at a pitch that was two feet outside. How did Wendt know? I wasn't yelling "steal" anymore. The kids had worked out pretty complex signals.

Even then, Carter beat the tag. But it was another one of those calls we weren't ever going to get. Sachs missed Carter only by a foot or two.

Like they do with major league stars, the umpires always gave the Maroons the "phantom" tags, and "phantom" double plays. When we were down 0–4, it seemed as if it could so easily have turned the other way. But it never did. It never would. It had all been a dream and we were being rudely awakened.

Maybe if Grand Rapids had beaten the Maroons and we had gone over the next day to play the remaining team, we *might* have done better. We might have gotten the "phantom" calls. But I seriously doubt it. My finesse game left much to be desired and we stuck out like the Kansas City Monarchs at the 1930 World Series—we simply didn't belong.

Game and tournament politics were the same in Connie Mack as they were in the NCAA, NFL, NBA, and the major leagues— the stars and the officials had an understanding. A player and a team *earned* its way to the "phantom" calls and championship performances. Bangor hadn't earned anything. We were a fringe team that had stumbled into the realpolitik of AABC tournament play without management/coaching/community support or money and influence. We were there without a clue.

These were not things to be taken lightly. A system was in place that took years to create, polish, and function smoothly. There was nothing unusual about this. From Little League to the major leagues *earning* the way to a championship took time, dedication, discipline, lots of hard work, and not a little politicking.

Bangor wasn't going to send anybody to the AABC Annual

Conference in Orlando and if we weren't going to be in Orlando we weren't going to be in the running.

Mike Hinga was State District Tournament director for many reasons and most had to do with hard work and commitment to the American Amateur Baseball Congress and the Maroons program he had built in Kalamazoo over the years.

It wasn't unfair. It was the way things were. Bangor had no more chance of winning the championship round than Mark Gola had of throwing more than five strikes to seven batters.

By the top of the fifth, we still hadn't scored a run. They hadn't scored on Billy and the score was still 0–4.

Maroons coach Barry Deal stopped by our dugout on his way to coach first. I had known Barry's older brother Wade in college. Wade had played football at Michigan State. "Why didn't you pitch him?" Barry pointed down to Josh Lute at third base. "He's a hell of a pitcher."

Pulling a confused look, I shrugged my shoulders. "Coaching decisions aren't in my job description. I am here mainly to take abuse and give strange looks to the umpires."

Barry laughed and walked on to his spot near the first base line. So the Maroons knew about Josh Lute. They must have also known something about Mark Gola; the umpires sure called his pitches like they did. Yet, Hinga had mentioned only Coleman.

The game seemed to play itself without us and by the bottom of the sixth we were down, 0–7. Except for Mark's "vanishing strike zone" in the first inning, Bangor had not done anything very bad. We just hadn't been able to do anything very good.

The Maroons continued to play their flawless brand of baseball. Nothing could be done to stop the inevitable, and, unless we could use handguns, our options were limited.

More than anything, I wanted the Bangor team overcoming all my mistakes, picking up their bootstraps and lifting themselves to an 8–7 comeback win. They should have pulled this game out in the last two innings like they had so many times before. The kids deserved a win like that. They had worked hard to reach the championships and I wish that they had pounded in eight runs and won the game in the bottom of the seventh. But wishes aren't horses—they're not even runs.

The game ended with the Maroons beating us, 0–7.

It was all over. It was over before it started. In two tournament games against the Maroons, we had not scored a single run.

The Maroons were a good team. You had to give them that. They consistently played well. Beating them for the district title and then advancing on to the Tristate Regional had always been a long shot and I had probably sealed our fate for sure by picking up so many new players to replenish our depleted roster.

Hinga controlled this district and he could overlook certain irregularities on my roster, especially since nobody turned in rosters from the Doubleheader League until the first day of the Districts—two weeks past the AABC deadline, a violation of rules that could cost the Maroons the district championship. Not well schooled in the AABC rules to know enough to "bend" them, I was particularly vulnerable to the finesse and subtlety that the uninitiated would call cheating. Hinga knew the rules inside and out. He could play them straight as railroad tracks, or twist them like pretzels. With ease, he could tie me up with the "rules" and still get me to agree that the knots were too loose.

The Maroons had outhit us, only 8–6. But, giving up five walks and four runs in the first inning set the tone. They scored seven runs and held us scoreless.

There was to be no Cinderella finish. Instead, I sat in the dugout and rapidly turned into a pumpkin as each inning passed.

"I haven't pitched in two years." I get a ringer in all the way from Chicago and don't even think to ask him when he last pitched.

Some of these kids hadn't even laid eyes on each other until yesterday and they still played an excellent power game. But against the Maroons that wasn't enough. And I had made bad decisions. In the three years we had been playing the Maroons, the only coaching decisions that helped us to a win were made by Carter.

After the game, the Bangor kids kept their heads up as they cleaned up the dugout and filled the equipment bags. Soon they began to discuss their plans for the rest of the day. It ended that quick. In the blink of an eye. The end of an era. The end of me as coach.

This morning I was.

This afternoon I was not.

44 ◇ The Fall

I COULD NOT GET my mind around the concept that something was changing in my life. Something that would affect me forever was tearing at my insides. Repressing it, I walked away from the field.

"Let's go, Dad," said Carter, walking toward the car. The bat bag was slung over his shoulder. The back of his neck was burnished a dark brown by the weeks in the summer sun.

Looking back at the field one last time to make certain we had not forgotten any equipment, I saw Mike Hinga talking to Billy Coleman near the home plate. The next week Coleman pitched a winning game for the Maroons in the Tristate Regional. He was a legitimate player as far as Hinga was concerned. Coleman had been on our roster for the Districts and I never told Mike he wasn't legitimate. That was why Mike had mentioned him. He wanted to make certain he could say I had claimed Coleman was a legal player and he could pick him up for the Regionals. Smiling, I shook my head. (Billy played for the Maroons the next summer and then, with Sachs, Yoshi Martin, and a couple of other Maroons, was playing for Western Michigan University's baseball team.)

"Toss me the keys, Dad," said Carter, waiting by the car with Mike Wisser, Steve Leonard, and Mike Wisniewski. All the equipment bags were stacked against the rear bumper. He grabbed the keys out of the air and bent to open the trunk. They quickly dumped the bags inside and Carter slammed the trunk shut, handing the keys back to me.

"I'm riding back with Steve, Dad," Carter said. "Is that all right? We may stop at Taco Bell in Paw Paw."

"Sure." I looked down and fiddled with the keys. "You all did a great job all season long. I was proud of you today. You guys ever get a real coach you could do something."

"It was fun, Dad, thanks." Carter hugged me. We patted each other on the back. I kissed him on the cheek. "The whole season was great."

Uninhibited, the others hugged me and thanked me. I knew they meant it and it meant a lot to me. They all piled into Steve's new red Ford Probe and drove off. I watched them until they disappeared around the Vicksburg High School building.

Nobody had even suggested I join them. Was it really over that fast? No more games. No more nothing. It was a long, lonely trip home, and as I drove, I relived the past years and months over and over. They had been the worst and best of times.

The Bangor Connie Mack teams had had tremendous seasons, beating teams from bigger towns with better-financed and -run programs. For the third straight time, these kids, who had started out all elbows and knees, had reached the AABC Connie Mack State District Tournament and had finally made it into the championship round. And for a bright, brief, white-hot moment, the Tristate Regional was within the grasp of little hillbilly Bangor. Who would have believed it?

Teams like Bangor were a rarity in the AABC Tristate Regional for the usual reason: money. The big cities controlled Connie Mack as a product with sponsors like Don Russ and Gatorade. The AABC held annual conferences for coaches and administrators in places like Orlando or Albuquerque. They marketed their product and their players just like the major leagues did. Budgets were astronomical. The Dallas Connie Mack team even had a private jet at their disposal.

Bangor's getting to the State Districts and beating Grand Rapids despite the loss of half of the original roster was a Herculean feat. The question of whether it was against the rules or not was another issue. Hinga thought we were within bounds and grabbed up Billy Coleman accordingly. In the Tristate Regional, the Maroons eventually lost to one of those *really-big-money* operations like Wendy's or Little Caesars or Salomon Brothers—I don't recall.

I was going to miss Carter and those other kids. They had been enchantment and bliss and transport. They had found me awash and drifting aimlessly every summer. Through baseball they gave me the energy to stay afloat, to take a few more strokes in search of the solid ground that had been eluding me since the early Eighties.

Now, left on my own, I would have to take responsibility for my life. I couldn't just tread water. I was going to have to swim with the sharks again, something I hadn't attempted in over a decade. I had no choice, it was swim or be chum of the day.

Living over half a century, setting goals, and working hard to accomplish them—from Bangor High School to Michigan State and the Dallas Cowboys—I had achieved nearly everything I had set out to do and nothing had worked out as I expected.

Spending years in the fast lane, crashing and burning and getting nowhere in a hurry, I had learned that control was delusion. If you were gonna wreck, you were gonna wreck. All you could do was what you could do.

Mostly, I ran aground, caught on fire, or came apart.

Life was a cruel sea, and except for those islands of time with Carter, I hadn't seen land in a decade.

45 ◇ Lucky Man

Until he is dead do not call a man happy, only lucky.
                                    —HERODOTUS I

SINCE THAT LONG-AGO championship game against the Maroons, it turned out 1993 would be the last magic summer. By the next year the world had turned many times and baseball had turned completely upside down.

The baseball strike cut short the 1994 season and there was no World Series. The 1995 season got started late and the playing showed it. Like lots of the fans, the magic was gone from baseball. The fans and the magic would probably return, eventually. Maybe not. Nothing turns out like you expect.

Carter graduated from high school in May 1994.

He was awarded the Bangor High School Student Athlete Award for achievements in athletics and in the classroom. Carter Gent would begin college at Western Michigan in the fall of 1994.

"Dad, I came by to get some posters for the house," Carter said, walking into my office. "Chris and I are gonna move some stuff up to Kalamazoo today." Chris Christian and Carter, who had been friends and had played summer baseball together since Carter moved back to Michigan in grade school, now were off to college together. It didn't seem possible.

Where had all that time gone? I was old. I looked old and felt old. When I got up in the morning it was as good as I felt all day. I had never sensed the loss of time so acutely as when I sat there watching Carter gathering up his possessions to move up to Kalamazoo where he would begin the next stage of his life.

"Are you taking anything from your grandmother's house?"

"Yeah, I'm taking some sheets and pillow cases," Carter said, peeling a poster of Michael Jordan defying gravity off the wall. He was moving out of the same house where I grew up, the very same room.

"I really don't have a lot of things to take," Carter said. "Except clothes. I got lots of clothes."

He was right about not having a lot of things. Getting out of Texas was such a desperate, costly, and hurried move that we had had to leave nearly everything we had behind. And, in the nine years we had been in Michigan, I had been unable to replace many things. Carter didn't have a CD player or a computer or the rest of the gear necessary for life in the twenty-first century.

All Carter had was an old Walkman and a great attitude. Life wasn't beating him down. He had fought the wars and emerged bloody but victorious. Carter was going to college. He was growing up, as I grew old. Older than my years. Carter was now moving away without me.

Time was a funny thing. All it did was run out.

46 ◇ Flawed Men

I sit alone thinking of a simpler time when all that mattered was that I felt good and that it wasn't raining. When the only words it seemed ever spoken were, "Hey, can't you play somewhere else?"

When the responsibilities were few if any, and it felt as if this time would never end, but it did and I miss it, too overanxious to enjoy and too regretful to remember.

Now at forty-five I have no games to play. I struggle to feed my children who this will happen to one day. But now my only escape is to think of a simpler time.

—CARTER GENT, *age twelve*

"DAD, WHY DID I have to graduate from high school?" Carter asked. I could feel him watching me as we drove east from Bangor. "If I am eating and I suddenly think about never playing baseball or basketball again, I lose my appetite," Carter continued. "I get sick. I have to play more. What should I do?"

"You have to think about the pros and cons of the next level of competition," I stalled. "Will you get out of it what you want. Only you can ever know that."

"I'll start thinking about playing high school ball and will actually believe I can go back and start it all again ... it is weird. Suddenly, I'll sort of come to and wonder what I thought I was doing. But there for a couple of minutes, I would actually believe I could go back in time." Carter wrung his hands.

"High school sports were good to me," I said to Carter. We were heading up Glendale Hill on our way to Kalamazoo to look at Western's campus and his house. "I just wanted the same for you."

"With your uncles and our friends," I said, "we won district and conference titles constantly. We won the 1960 State Basketball Championship."

"I'll bet that was fresh." Carter smiled. "I just can't imagine what that would feel like."

"It was the most incredible experience in sports. Nothing touched it from Michigan State to the NFL," I said. "Things were just never the same after high school. I wanted high school sports to be great for you. I am sorry that the coaches and administrators ruined it for you."

"We had good baseball teams," Carter said. "During school and in the summers. I loved baseball because we won. We never won at anything else."

"You deserved better. You are a skillful player and you improve at such a tremendous rate," I said. "You're the kind of athlete good coaches dream about. They say it once. You remember it forever. Unfortunately, you've never had a good coach."

"We started out so well in basketball," Carter said, the disappointment filled his voice.

"You should have had a big year in basketball," I said. "You were averaging twenty points a game and getting better each game."

"I thought we could win the conference," Carter said.

"Bangor was five of six and ranked in the state," I said. "Then the jerk tells you to stop shooting. The team only wins five more games all season."

"I don't know." Carter was saddened by thoughts of the missed opportunities. "I was feeling so good about playing, until he started yelling at me." Yelling at the kids was not one of the mistakes I made.

Carter's high school basketball coach thought he was the next Bobby Knight. Bobby publicly humiliated his players on television; this coach did it in Bangor. This was a coach who thought the game was about *him* and not about the players. He talked about his goals of winning a state championship, then winning an NCAA title and, finally, topping it all off with an NBA World Championship.

A kid not yet twenty-five, he had no idea of the work and talent necessary to succeed at the high school level, let alone the NCAA and the NBA. This was the guy coaching Carter, and every game he engaged in the abuse of the whole team.

After one early-season loss, he called a Saturday team meeting and made the kids watch the movie *Hoosiers.* He cried at the end of it. This guy needed to get back to Planet Earth, but he just kept drifting farther and farther away. By Carter's senior year, he was reaching outer space and the season that began so well became a nightmare. In their sixth game Carter scored thirty points to lead Bangor to its fifth win and Bangor's first state ranking in years. I remember the game like it happened yesterday. It was better than playing myself.

The game went down to the wire with Carter and Fennville's all-state guard exchanging three pointers. Carter hit six for the night and Bangor won by a single point.

I had expected Carter to be good, but his improvement over the previous year was phenomenal. One of the top scorers in the area, Carter was just beginning to hit his stride. He knew that the game was played in his head and had excellent concentration and focus. As a player, Carter would never peak; he would just learn more and get better continually. All Carter needed was a coach.

With the death of that season died Carter's dreams. So much had seemed within his grasp, only to be yanked away by his "coach." He had cost Carter a promising career in high school basketball and any chance at scholarship offers or even just college interest.

"I'm thinking about trying to play in college." Carter's voice brought me back to the here and now. I had been watching the road and driving on autopilot.

I had hoped high school would be enough for Carter. But now I had to convey the pitfalls of the next level to him. It would not be easy. How could I convince Carter that there were worse coaches than his high school coach at the college level? "College ball wasn't fun like high school. Playing at State was a job," I said. "Don't ever forget that. It's all different after high school. Coaches are more desperate and dangerous."

"I would like a chance at a job like that," Carter replied. "I want to play college ball."

"You probably can. A good coach will see your talent, if you get a good coach and he bothers to look," I said. "But I never really had the experience of going to college. I just played ball and, when I could, attended class. I missed a lot."

"Yeah," Carter replied. "But you got to do things most people only dream of doing."

"Maybe that was the problem," I replied. "When I was playing it seemed like a dream."

"Do you really think I could play in college?" Carter studied my face. "The truth, really?"

"Yeah, really," I said. "But college programs are afflicted with the same viruses that kill high school programs: coaches. You've got to accept injuries and humiliation as givens."

"So you think I could play?"

"Sure. But talent is only part of the equation. It was the same after my first season with Dallas," I said. "Professional football was exciting. The players were incredibly talented, tough, and fascinating men. And like me, they were flawed, damaged men with world-class athletic skill, capable of grand passions. Love and hate. Anybody can love, you got to be really tough to hate. These were really tough guys."

"What does that have to do with playing basketball in college?" Carter frowned. He thought I was avoiding his question. I was and I wasn't.

"It is a decision that affects your whole life," I said. "Before I made the decision to continue on with a career in professional football, I had to take the winter of 1965 to rethink my whole approach to life."

"Why?" Carter was surprised. We had never discussed sport in such murky detail before. "What was the big deal?"

"I knew that to build a career in the NFL I would have to become a different person," I replied. "Playing in the NFL wasn't what I did, it was what I was. My life changed forever. I was traveling faster than I could see."

"But," Carter asked, "you were glad you did it?"

"Yeah, because the end result is the now of sitting here with you," I replied. "But is it the life I would choose for you?"

"The choice isn't up to you anymore," Carter said.

◇

After taking clothes to Carter's new house in Kalamazoo, we arrived back in Bangor to find my brother Jamie visiting with his family. Carter immediately enlisted his uncle Jamie in the discussion of sports beyond high school.

"Well, Carter is certainly good enough to play at any of the smaller colleges," Jamie said. "He ought to check that out."

"I want to play, somewhere," said Carter, so obviously unhappy over the end of his sports career that it was depressing to watch. Yet, I was so confused about the value of college sport, I did not know how to help him.

"He's already set at Western. I don't like the idea of choosing a college because some coach promises you can play ball there," I said. "Coaches will promise anything as long as keeping the promise isn't necessary."

"Maybe a few years more of playing ball is more important than anything," Jamie offered. "You only get to do this once and at his age a few more years is a lot."

"I just want to keep playing, just to play." Carter was irritated by my constant cautioning. "It is my decision to play or not, right?"

"Maybe you should just walk on at Western. You've got Division I skills," I said. Confused by my attitude, I ran my hand through Carter's thick hair and wondered what was right.

"Yeah," Carter said. "But look at me. I've got no upper body."

"Basketball is contact and strength." I nodded. "But it is also finesse and brains. You're as smart a high school player as I've seen. You have to make up for your physical size."

"Well, what should I do?" Carter looked from Jamie to me.

"Play if you want to," Jamie said. "Don't let any coach discourage you. If I'd listened to my coaches I never would have played at Central Michigan. If your dad had listened he would have never left Bangor."

"And look what I got for leaving Bangor," I said. I looked at Carter. "You know how I feel about sports after high school. I . . . I am worried about what it really is and does." I was worried that the next generation of good men would have little chance to flourish in the big-college and pro-sport atmosphere. I saw the damage of the "trickle-down effect" of big-time sports to high school and junior high school programs. "It will be a difficult decision," I said.

"Yeah," Jamie added. "But it is his difficult decision. You and I played at the college level and look how we turned out."

I turned and just stared at my younger brother.

"Maybe that was a poor example." Jamie grinned.

"Do I want Carter to go through what you and I did?" I asked him.

"That's the unanswerable question," Jamie replied. "He is not you or me and it is not thirty plus years ago."

"Jamie, I had some of the best basketball and football coaches in the country." I shook my head in despair. "Still, it was like a full moon at the madhouse most of the time."

"But, like Carter," Jamie replied, "you really did love to play and maybe that was all that mattered."

Jamie was right.

Thirty-five years later I still dream that I am young, fast, and smart, and feel no pain. That I can still hit a thirty-foot jump shot with ease or make a two-fingered catch of the winning TD pass against Green Bay. The dreams are so real, I enjoy the memory of them long after the pain in my body has awakened me to the real world of travail and heartache—but never regret—I have made for myself.

And when I watched Carter play, something from the murky depths of my soul *did* want Carter to play at the next level. And be not just a player, but *the player*. I wanted Carter to have it all. Because I knew one thing about sports, professional and amateur, when it all went right—in the zone and unbeatable— it was a rapturous high bestowed by the gods.

So many times in his life, I had been unable to give Carter the things he would have liked. It was teaching Carter needed now. His capacity and ability to learn were immense. Once Carter learned the art of visualization—he could be *the player*. Great athletes harness chaos theory by visualization. Chaos was the force, and by visualizing, the great player had already played the game in all its variations before he arrived at the stadium.

But, I couldn't teach Carter how to visualize. Only days, weeks, and months of demonstration and repetition of execution could increase a player's ability to visualize effectively. To teach Carter the necessary physical skills and fundamental techniques required grace, balance, ease of movement. My body was no longer capable of this delicate footwork and motion.

It would be like trying to teach Tai Chi from an iron lung. My unique athletic experience would forever remain anecdotal. The truly rare athletic talents I had spent years developing were now irrelevant. My body was a husk. I could not move. My skills were abstractions. My life one long skull session.

Now, I understood clearly that the good day to die was close. Carter only had so many years to play. So many years of being in the moment. Being here and doing it now. And, I did not know how much longer I had left to watch.

"I've just got to play, Dad," Carter said.

"I know what you're feeling," I said. "But just remember that being a star college or pro athlete isn't a reward for a job well done. It's your punishment for believing that doing the job well was going to get you a reward."

Carter stared at me, momentarily, then frowned and shook his head in dismay at my attitude. "Be careful what you wish for?" he asked me.

"Yeah." I nodded. "That and live every day as if it was your last."

"You're not much help." Carter frowned again. His brown hair fell across his high forehead. "I need answers."

"Or better questions." I chewed on my upper lip. "Carter, I swear to God, I do not know if there is a right answer."

Was big-time sport really that Kafkaesque? Was this high-tech playground too dangerous for my unprotected son? Was I selling him short?

"It all seems so different than when I played," I said. "Now the boundaries between players, owners, and the media aren't very clear. Big money has made everybody crazy."

"High school and college kids are coming onto the sports market like cattle," Jamie pointed out. "I see it in Lansing and Detroit all the time. Hell, the sale of a grade school or junior high kid is not unusual." After a thirty-year career in athletics and education, Jamie was dismayed. "Parents sell their kids to high school coaches in Detroit," Jamie said. "Because the private and public schools allow kids to come from anywhere. Then, the parents and coaches sell the kids to colleges. Then, they do it again come the pro-drafts."

The new communications information moguls were wrestling for the best lanes on the Info-Highway. A lot of the software and programming was going to be sports from American gladiators to college and pro teams. Did I want Carter playing in the traffic?

47 ◇ Gone

IN APRIL 1995, CARTER finished his freshman year at college. We don't see each other much. Not like before, when we used to see each other every day and night. When I woke him up in the morning and tucked him in at night, and if he was sick or scared, when he would sleep with me.

I seem to see him less and less as he speeds up and crippled old age grinds me to a stop.

Thinking of those long-ago days, when he played Tee Ball in Texas and I battled my ex-wife and Judge Warner for the right to play catch and watch his games, I realized that real-life disasters do not recognize sticking to the baselines, or the necessity of keeping the playing field free of greed and vengeance.

Through those difficult years, I watched him grow and heal on the playing field. I watched the beneficial joy of baseball for him. The game restored a wholeness to his life and a belief in his own abilities as a young man. Playing and losing himself in the world of the game, Carter grew into a complete person and a good baseball player.

But thankful as I was for baseball's redemptive and salubrious effects on my son as he grew up, still it took me a long, long time to regain the necessary perspective to fathom Carter's love for and fascination with college and professional sports. Though it was a strange contradiction in our lives, I eventually learned how to enjoy and benefit from it. Carter taught me. Slowly but surely sports on the other level became another language between us.

During the worst of times, communication had always been very important and one of our strongest bonds. The additional parlance of sport increased our understanding of each other and our comprehension of what our struggles had meant. And while our deepest emotional bonds always would be welded by the terrors of divorce and custody, we had bonded more and more in the gentle joy of baseball.

I taught Carter how to think it and play it and he broke through my hard shell of anger and my fear of the demons of sport. Finally, he resurrected my life, allowing me to take pride in my accomplishments and to forgive all my real or imaginary transgressions against myself. Years of studying Carter's great heart and athletic spirit, his generous ability to appreciate skill in others, began to show me how to age gracefully. In my rage I had forgotten my heart and buried it somewhere.

We are born alone and we die alone. But Carter taught me to appreciate all those years in between. Those years from Bangor to Michigan State and the Dallas Cowboys and back to Bangor and summer baseball where we lived and died as a team.

A while back, we were watching the ESPN *Sports Awards Show*, lying side by side on the couch. With Alex at his feet, Carter rested his head on my chest and stared in wide-eyed wonder at a particularly spectacular video montage of basketball, baseball, and football plays. He turned and smiled up at me.

"Sports are just amazing, aren't they, Dad?" His voice was filled with awe and admiration.

They are.

But for me they are also just too crazy to completely comprehend. I was still not sure I wanted Carter around those people. Heroic character cannot survive in the hothouse atmosphere of avarice and self-absorption that permeates the college and professional locker rooms and front offices. What can Carter learn from those guys except how *not* to behave? I wanted to tell him to walk away from big-time sports and not look back unless he wanted to become a salt lick.

But, I couldn't. It was his turn.

If Carter really wanted to play, he would find a way.

I had made my mistakes and Carter had heard about every one of them. Over and over.

Now, the world belonged to Carter.

48 ◇ The Dugout

LATE THIS LAST FALL, I went down to the Bangor High School baseball diamond. I sat alone in the dugout.

Carter was gone. All the boys were gone.

The sky was a cobalt blue and the sun hung low enough in the southern sky to warm me while the cement block walls shielded me from any wind.

The sky was pocked with those damn birds, the birds that had so long ago endangered my young players by entrancing them into taking their eyes off the baseball to watch them flit through the air.

Supposedly learning the basics of defense out in the field, the kids twisted their little bodies back and forth, chewed on their glove laces, and watched the birds winging overhead. Those who weren't birdwatching might be on their knees in the outfield looking for four leaf clovers or have their backs completely turned on the batter watching the five o'clock freight from Chicago to Grand Rapids.

The kids I was remembering were grown and gone. Long gone. They would never look or be like that again. Without them the dugout was shabby, the inside littered with smashed paper cups, sunflower seed bags, a few old cigarette butts, two plastic Gatorade bottles, crumpled Red Man chewing tobacco bags, and several Skoal Bandit snuff cans.

Behind the dugout bench, jammed into a notch in the cement blocks, I found the old lineup card from the second Maroons regular-season doubleheader, when we hammered them, 8–2, behind Carter's coaching, Mike Wisniewski's pitching, and Mike Wisser's grand slam home run.

The lineup card made me smile. That was worth something.

The field seemed poorly kept and forgotten. Looking down the right-field line, over the fence west to the horizon and Lake Michigan, I could see the deep blue sky broken by the ever-present steam cloud that billowed white from the cooling tower of the Palisades Nuclear Power Plant.

One of the most dangerous nuclear plants in the United States was eight miles upwind, sending every release of radiation drifting right over the school buildings, recess yards, parking lots, and athletic fields of the Bangor public schools. And I had brought Carter here to keep him safe. The view was madness itself.

But, death did not figure in the equation of baseball, where nothing but the game mattered. The wisdom that death was what made life real had not yet been revealed.

That every man had a last season, a last summer, was yet to be considered by young men with such passions and appetites. They were athletes infused with the great psychosis of sport. The self-delusion of the big-league dream.

I had spent eight years coaching summer baseball. Those kids had kept me young, soothed my soul with laughter and their wild race into the future. Now they were off in college or at work, struggling to make their marks outside of Bangor where people just might appreciate their efforts more.

Sitting in the dugout that day, I heard their voices calling me.

Though I knew my ears and the wind were playing tricks, I still heard those kids, clearly, calling from the field in their mismatched uniforms.

It was never going to happen again. Ever.

Early in my divorce, this same phenomenon used to visit me regularly, especially in crowded airports or hotel lobbies when I was on book tours or traveling to do television shows.

"Dad!" Carter would be calling out to me from somewhere in the bustling crowd. "Hey, Dad!"

I would turn and look, knowing all the while he couldn't possibly be there. He was back in Texas with his mother.

Yet I would hear that unmistakable voice. "Hey, Dad, wait up." Where was he? I would scan the crowded terminal or lobby for his face.

And today? I am at peace with the realization that life is the trip not the destination and I am thankful for my part in my son's ride to adulthood. As I watch all the boys grow up and Carter become a man, I know his need for my help and company will lessen with each day . . . and, as much as I'll miss him, I wouldn't want it any other way.

Carter has accepted the responsibilities of a man for so many years that his passage into manhood seems redundant. Yet, in other ways, he still seems that little boy who was living in the wonder and joy of a child's world when it blew up in his face.

He was only six years old.

So long ago.

EPILOGUE

The Magician

"The best thing for being sad," replied Merlyn, beginning to puff and blow, "is to learn something. That is the only thing that never fails. You may grow old and trembling in your anatomies, you may lie awake at night listening to the disorder of your veins, you may miss your only love, you may see the world about you devastated by evil lunatics, or know your honour trampled in the sewers of baser minds. There is only one thing for it then—to learn. Learn why the world wags and what wags it. That is the only thing which the mind can never exhaust, never alienate, never be tortured by, never fear or distrust, and never dream of regretting."

—T. H. WHITE